All About
CANDLESTICK
CHARTING

THE EASY WAY TO GET STARTED

OTHER TITLES IN THE "ALL ABOUT" FINANCE SERIES

All About
CANDLESTICK
CHARTING

THE EASY WAY TO GET STARTED

WAYNE A. CORBITT

New York Chicago San Francisco Lisbon London Madrid
Mexico City Milan New Delhi San Juan Seoul
Singapore Sydney Toronto

To Jaime
Your smile lights up my life

1 2 3 4 5 6 7 8 9 10 DOC/DOC 1 9 8 7 6 5 4 3 2 1

ISBN: 978-0-07-176312-7
MHID: 0-07-176312-0

e-ISBN: 978-0-07-176313-4
e-MHID: 0-07-176313-9

This publication is designed to provide accurate and authoritative information in regard to the subject matter covered. It is sold with the understanding that neither the author nor the publisher is engaged in rendering legal, accounting, securities trading, or other professional services. If legal advice or other expert assistance is required, the services of a competent professional person should be sought.
    —*From a Declaration of Principles Jointly Adopted by a Committee of the American Bar Association and a Committee of Publishers and Associations*

Library of Congress Cataloging-in-Publication Data

Corbitt, Wayne A.
  All about candlestick charting / by Wayne A. Corbitt.
     p. cm.
  ISBN-13: 978-0-07-176312-7 (alk. paper)
  ISBN-10: 0-07-176312-0 (alk. paper)
  1. Stocks--Charts, diagrams, etc. 2. Investment analysis. I. Title.
  HG4638.C67 2012
  332.63'2042--dc23

                                                                    2011027719

CONTENTS

PART 3: CANDLESTICK COUSINS: OTHER CHARTING METHODS

INTRODUCTION

Arm yourself. These two words have never been more appropriate for trading and investing than they are today. Knowledge is power, especially when it comes to investing your hard-earned money. Even with the exposure of Wall Street criminals (Madoff, Sanford, et al.), financial gimmickry (QE1 and QE2), and high-frequency trading, the markets still have enough quality to allow the average person to participate in an effort to build and protect his or her wealth. Whether you trade your own money or have a trusted advisor watching over your funds, this book can be of use to you. Employing the techniques presented here will help you gain more confidence in trading your own account or allow you to have an informed conversation about the position of the markets with your money manager.

Candlestick charting has been around for centuries and really does shed more light on the mindset of traders than do the other standard charting methods. This book is not about laying out a hard and fast trading system with rigid rules. Some rules always must be followed when it comes to managing risk, but by combining Western technical analysis with candlestick patterns, you should be able to develop your own trading system. It is my intention to lay a basic foundation of the principles of both candlestick charting and technical analysis to allow you to take this knowledge as far as you want to go with it. My favorite technical analysis books over the years have been those which planted seeds that allowed me to try my own ideas and come up with my own way of doing things. I hope this book will do that for you.

Before we begin the journey into candlestick charting, I would like to acknowledge some of the good people in the industry whose legacies will far outweigh the blemishes of the crooks named above. Constance Brown, whose work has inspired me to dig deeper with her fantastic knowledge base and writing style, is one of the truly great teachers in the industry today. Martin Pring is a living legend in the technical analysis industry and has done extensive work with momentum indicators. Greg Morris, whom I had the pleasure of meeting in October 2010 in Las Vegas, is a true gentleman and family man. His down-to-earth demeanor is refreshing in an industry filled with egos and self-promotion. Greg's work with candlesticks in the 1990s also helped pave the way for people like me to pick up this superior charting methodology and share it with others. Last but not least I would like to acknowledge Mark Leibovit, whom I have known for over seven years. Mark's work with volume is viewed by many as the gold standard in the industry. I first began working with Mark by utilizing my programming background to help develop trading signals for his systems and perform daily data runs to assist with his daily market analysis. Mark also asked me to assist him on his recently released book, *The Trader's Book of Volume*, which was quite an undertaking but well worth the effort. The experiences I have had with Mark have helped me grow professionally.

The work of Steve Nison must be acknowledged in any book about Japanese candlesticks as his research and perseverance helped integrate candlestick charting into Western technical analysis. Without Mr. Nison's work, candlestick charting would be nowhere near the level of popularity it has achieved today. If you have never used the candlestick charting method or if, like me at one time, you look at it as a novelty, your eyes will be opened as we step through the basics of candlestick construction, candlestick types, and candlestick pattern analysis and show how the effectiveness of candlestick patterns can be enhanced by combining them with more contemporary Western technical analysis tools.

PART 1

Candlesticks: Their Construction and Patterns

CHAPTER 1

The Illuminating Power of the Candle

For centuries the candle has been used to illuminate our surroundings. Without light, simple tasks such as walking across a familiar room become much more difficult. Maybe you are new to trading or maybe you have been trading for a while. In either case, if you feel like you are lost or groping in the dark when it comes to making solid trading decisions, this book is for you. My goal is to show you how the extra layer of analysis provided by candlestick charting can allow you to see the markets in a whole new light. The concepts discussed in this book will be of benefit to traders of all time frames and temperaments. Whether you realize it or not, everyone is a trader because every trade has to have an entry and an exit. Some trades may be entered into and exited from in the same day, whereas others may be held for weeks, months, or even years. Together we will build from a foundation of candlestick patterns and add different indicators to enhance your odds for trading success. This journey will demonstrate the value of Japanese candlestick charting and allow you to apply the concepts presented here to read the subtle signals given by the market every single trading day. Although most of the examples in this book involve daily charts, these concepts can be used in any time frame, from intraday to monthly.

Japanese candlestick charts were developed in Japan over 200 years ago but have become a standard charting methodology in Western culture only over the last 20 years, largely as a result of the work of Steve Nison and Greg Morris. Munehisa Honma developed candlestick charting around 1750 to analyze price movements at his local rice market in Sakata. Honma's efforts allowed him to accumulate vast wealth while becoming a legendary trader. The culture in Honma's day was heavily influenced by the military. Throughout the book you will notice that candlestick charting employs many militaristic terms, which makes it similar to battle scenarios. Success in a military campaign requires planning, patience, discipline, and unwavering execution. These are also traits of the most successful traders in the financial markets.

This ancient methodology has an advantage over more modern Western charting styles because of its appealing appearance and ability to show intraday data relationships effectively, most notably the relationship between the opening and closing prices. A *dark* (or filled) candle body shows that the closing price was lower than the opening price, and a *white* (or hollow) candle body shows that the closing price was higher than the opening price. Figure 1-1 illustrates how candlestick colors show the relationship between the opening and closing prices. These differences in appearance can give a trader a quick report on whether the efforts of buyers were stronger than those of sellers or vice versa for the time period being examined, whether it is intraday, daily, weekly, or monthly.

FIGURE 1-1

Candles and the Open-Close Price Relationship

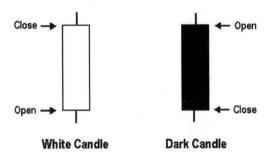

White Candle   Dark Candle

The simple open-close relationship creates the foundation for more complex and revealing analysis. Groups of candlesticks, or candlestick *patterns*, are also easily identifiable and have unique names such as dark cloud cover, three white soldiers, and counterattack lines. Once you unlock the wealth of information that is available in a candlestick chart, I am confident that it will become your first choice among charting styles. Before we dig deeper into candlesticks, let's lay the groundwork for later sections of the book that blend the ancient art of candlestick charting with the more modern Western discipline of technical analysis.

WHAT IS TECHNICAL ANALYSIS AND WHY SHOULD YOU USE IT?

The writings of Charles Dow around the turn of the twentieth century provided the foundation from which modern technical analysis has evolved. Dow's early writings constituted what is now known as Dow theory.

Modern technical analysis is based on the following principles:

1. The market discounts everything that can affect the price of a security.
2. Prices are driven by the expectations of market participants.
3. Price movements are not totally random.
4. What price did is more important than why it did it.
5. History tends to repeat itself.

The Market Discounts Everything That Can Affect the Price of a Security

Technicians believe that the current price level of any security is based on the collective knowledge of all market participants. Those participants represent a broad array of investment styles and methodologies used by technical analysts, fundamental analysts, institutions, and portfolio managers, among others. This melting pot of approaches and opinions provides what amounts to a fair price for a security.

Prices Are Driven by the Expectations of Market Participants

Prices are affected by the consensus of opinion among buyers and sellers. These opinions or expectations for future price growth drive decisions made to buy or sell a security. These collective actions provide the foundation for *trends*, or the tendency of price to move in one direction over time. Trends are covered in Chapter 5.

Price Movements Are Not Totally Random

If price movements were totally random, it would be virtually impossible to make money by using any form of rational market analysis. Using technical analysis over different time frames can identify times when shares are being accumulated or distributed by major institutions. This concept dovetails with the previous point about the expectations of market participants. If expectations are favorable, systematic accumulation should be visible as price makes higher highs and higher lows. Conversely, if expectations are unfavorable, systematic distribution should be visible as price makes lower highs and lower lows.

What Price Did Is More Important Than Why It Did It

Building on the concepts outlined above, it stands to reason that if price action discounts all available news, represents the collective outlook of market participants, and shows systematic accumulation or distribution of shares, all necessary information should be reflected in the direction and magnitude of price moves. A true technician does his or her best to block out news and opinions and concentrate solely on charts.

History Tends to Repeat Itself

Technical analysis captures the mood or sentiment of market participants. By looking for specific price and volume patterns, technicians can develop reasonable expectations for future price movement.

By using a disciplined approach that is based on these principles, a trader can develop a sound trading system that yields profits. Technical analysis is based on expectations that are based on *expected outcomes*, not hard and fast predictions. The goal of technical analysis is not to be right 100 percent of the time but to alert a trader to high-probability opportunities for profit that can be exploited in the market.

TECHNICAL ANALYSIS MEASURES SUPPLY AND DEMAND

Many insults have been hurled at market technicians over the years by those who do not understand the simplicity of price and volume plots. Technical analysis has been referred to as reading chicken entrails, reading tea leaves, and, one of my favorites, reading squiggles. What these uninformed souls fail to recognize is that in its simplest form, technical analysis measures the supply and demand of the security being charted.

There is no other method I know of that captures the supply and demand picture of a security better than a price and volume chart. Supply and demand form the foundation of *support* and *resistance* lines, as will be discussed in Chapter 5. Price constantly adjusts in the market because of the ever-changing forces of supply and demand. Excess supply of a security means that there are more sellers than buyers, which causes price to move lower until demand increases. If demand is strong but there are fewer sellers at a particular price, then price will rise to reflect the excess demand.

A key component of supply and demand analysis is volume, or the number of shares or contracts that changed hands during a specific time period. Volume is used to measure the validity of a price move. The higher the volume is when price moves, the more meaning the price move has. Volume will be discussed in more detail in Chapter 7.

Figure 1-2 shows a move higher in price on increasing volume. Buyer demand was stronger than the overhead supply of shares, and that pushed price higher. The increase in volume showed that there was strong passion among buyers, who were willing to pay higher prices to own shares of Apple in July 2009. Notice how price continued to rise for the next two months.

FIGURE 1-2

Supply and Demand for Apple Inc., Daily

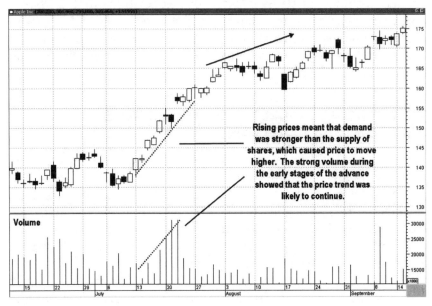

Rising prices meant that demand was stronger than the supply of shares, which caused price to move higher. The strong volume during the early stages of the advance showed that the price trend was likely to continue.

Source: MetaStock

TECHNICAL ANALYSIS ADDRESSES MARKET RISK

The term *risk* refers to the possibility of capital loss or less than expected investment returns. Risk often is confused with *volatility,* which measures the size of the variance of price movement for a security or index. Investment risk is a very complex topic as it manifests itself in many different forms, such as inflation risk, principal risk, liquidity risk, and valuation risk. This book concentrates on two types of risk. *Market risk* is defined as the chance that the broader market could go down in value, adversely affecting the value of investments. If the risk categories were divided into pieces of a pie, market risk would represent the largest slice. This was evidenced by the 2008 market meltdown, in which market classes that normally have low correlation all fell in unison. We also will address *trading risk,* which is the amount of possible loss on each individual trade. Trading risk will be addressed through the use of stop loss orders.

Since most stocks tend to move in the direction of the overall market, knowing the overall market trend can keep a trader properly positioned. Just as fighting a strong river current is very difficult if not impossible, so is fighting the current of institutional money that flows into or out of the market. Figure 1-3 shows how even the simplest trend-following systems can address general market risk. From March 2003 to October 2007, the S&P 500 was in an *uptrend* as it made a series of higher highs and higher lows. The lows are connected with a *trendline* that when violated signals that the uptrend is in danger of reversing. Once the trendline was crossed to the downside in October 2007, a signal was given that market risk had increased and it was time to reduce long side exposure. This was also a signal for more aggressive traders to

FIGURE 1-3

Weekly Trendline Violation: S&P 500 Index

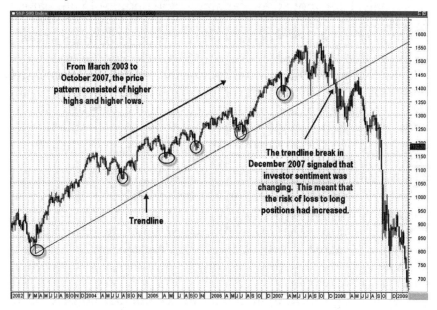

Source: MetaStock

begin looking at *short* trades, or trades that increase in value as the prices of equities fall.

In Chapters 5 and 6 we zoom in on the 2007 top in the S&P 500 to look at specific short-term clues given by the candlestick pattern that provided an earlier warning that a change of trend, or price direction, was occurring in the market. The synergy generated by combining the ancient methodologies of Japanese candlestick charting with more modern Western technical analysis techniques provides a deeper look into market behavior and will increase the odds of your trading success.

MASTERING TECHNICAL ANALYSIS TAKES MUCH PRACTICE

Becoming a good technician is much more difficult than loading up charting software, plotting price with a momentum indicator, and making market calls. In fact, it is behavior like this that gives seasoned technical analysts a bad name. I am appalled at some of the material on the Internet that is labeled as technical analysis. Using price momentum indicators does not mean you are a technical analyst any more than standing in the middle of your garage means you are a car.

Analyzing the markets properly is a product of trial and error until you find the right fit for your trading style. For example, those who trade stocks in small intraday time increments can concentrate on setups in individual names. Conversely, those who trade with the intention of holding an equity position for weeks or months need to give more weight to the complexion of the overall market since the moves of the overall market tend to take individual stocks along for the ride.

Technical analysis is a valid discipline and should be treated as such. A global organization for those interested in technical analysis is the Market Technicians Association (MTA), of which I am a member. The MTA certifies its members through its Chartered Market Technician (CMT) Program, which consists of three tests that are designed to prove proficiency in technical analysis of the markets.

Achieving certification is only the beginning, however. The market is a living, breathing entity that feeds on trader losses. The more prepared you are to do battle with the market, the better chance you will have of trading success. When you are developing your own methodology for analyzing the market, remember to address as broad a picture as possible while striving to keep your methodology as simple as possible. I have seen some very complex systems that look and sound impressive until the market takes an unexpected turn that causes those methodologies to crash and burn. The fact that a system looks good on paper does not guarantee its success when real bullets are flying during the trading day.

Although candlestick setups and trades are typically patterns that affect the short term (a week or less), those short-term reversals or continuations can lead to much larger moves. Those of you who are position traders (days, weeks, months) can increase the odds of holding a winning position when you incorporate broader market analysis into your candlestick analysis.

COMMON CHARTING STYLES

Technical analysis involves the use of price charts. A *chart* is a tool used by technicians to display price information about a security graphically. Three of the four charting styles we will show include a plot of volume as well. Choosing a charting style is a personal decision. A trader needs to look at a chart display that he or she is comfortable with and that gives him or her the most information in as little time as possible. Each of the chart examples listed below will show the same security (Google) over the same time frame (November 2009–May 2010) to allow for valid comparisons. We will concentrate on four popular charting styles that technicians use:

1. Line
2. Point and figure
3. Bar
4. Candlestick

Line Chart

A line chart displays only the closing price for each time period, with that price connected by a single line. Some traders are concerned only with the closing price since that price contains the sum of all activity during the trading day, with the rest of the day's

FIGURE 1-4

Line Chart for Google Inc., Daily

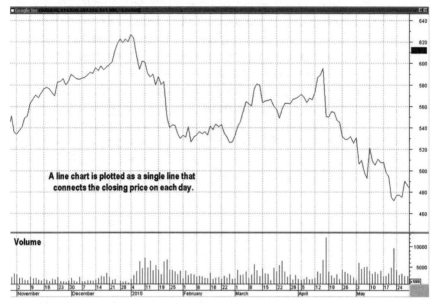

Source: MetaStock

activity being nothing more than "noise." By using a line chart, a trader can miss out on seeing where price may have reversed during the trading day, which provides valuable information about where support or resistance may be in price movement. Figure 1-4 shows a line chart.

Point and Figure Chart

Point and figure charts consist of columns of X's and O's that represent price movements. This charting methodology uses the high and/or low price of the day in its construction; therefore, it is focused more on the daily extremes than on the closing price. The benefits of this charting methodology are that it shows support and resistance levels more clearly and also makes for easier drawing and interpretation of trendlines. There are a couple of drawbacks to using a point and figure chart. First, its construction

FIGURE 1-5

Point and Figure Chart for Google Inc., Daily

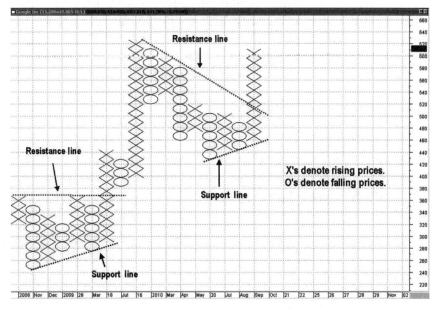

Source: MetaStock

is concerned only with price movements above or below price levels regardless of *when* they occur. This eliminates the property of time, which is very important to those who do any form of time cycle analysis. Second, its construction eliminates the use of volume as a valuable measure of trader sentiment behind price moves. In spite of these drawbacks, point and figure charting is still popular with many market technicians. Figure 1-5 shows a point and figure chart. There are other Japanese charting methods that are based on the same concepts; they will be presented in Chapters 9, 10, and 11.

Bar Chart

The bar chart is perhaps the most commonly used form of charting and has been the industry standard for years. With candlestick charting increasing in popularity, however, the bar chart's status as the industry standard may be changing.

A bar chart consists of bars for each trading period (Figure 1-6 shows daily bars) that consist of the open, high, low, and close for a session. Bar charts contain much more information than line or point and figure charts. This methodology also allows for the proper plotting of volume for each time period, which adds another layer to market analysis. Figure 1-6 shows a daily bar chart.

A bar chart can show where price opened for any time period and where it closed. This price relationship shows whether buying or selling pressure was stronger for that day.

Bar charts also show price *gaps*, or blank spots on charts where no trading occurred between the close of one bar and the opening of the next bar. These are emotional events that normally are tied to earnings reports, news stories surrounding a particular stock, or simply broad market news.

FIGURE 1-6

Bar Chart for Google Inc., Daily

Source: MetaStock

Candlestick Chart

A candlestick chart takes the bar chart one step farther by enhancing the all-important open-close relationship during the trading day. The visual aspects of candlesticks almost jump off the page at a trader, offering much more "at a glance" information than can be gleaned from a standard bar chart. Figure 1-7 shows the same price plot as the bar chart in Figure 1-6, but note how much more discernible the daily patterns are because of the contrast between dark and white candles. Most candlestick charting packages show candlesticks with different colors, but for the purposes of this book black candles will be used on days when the close is lower than the open, and white candles will be used when the close is higher than the open. Also notice how the three tops shown in the chart were marked by reversal candles such as the doji, spinning top,

FIGURE 1-7

Candlestick Chart for Google Inc., Daily

Source: MetaStock

and dark cloud cover. Each of these candlestick formations and the psychology behind them will be discussed in more detail in Chapter 3.

Candlestick charts also show price gaps just as bar charts do, only in candlestick charting, gaps are referred to as *windows* that are opened and closed by price action. Note the two windows in Figure 1-7. An upside gap is referred to as a *rising window,* and a downside gap is referred to as a *falling window.*

Candlestick charting has three distinct advantages over bar charts:

1. **Readability.** Candlestick charts provide more insight into the all-important open-close relationship. Although this is a short-term phenomenon, it can alert a trader to a possible change in market psychology that could lead to a price trend reversal.

2. **Easier and faster interpretation of the market.** Are there more black candles than white candles? That alone can tell a trader whether a stock or index is under accumulation or distribution. Reversal and continuation patterns are spotted more readily because of the color or shading contrasts between positive and negative days. Referring again to Figure 1-7, notice how a doji, a dark cloud cover, and a spinning top marked the three high points on the chart. Would those patterns be spotted as easily on a bar chart?

3. **Specific patterns give insight into market psychology.** For example, if a doji is formed at a low and is followed by a long white candle, that is a sign that sentiment among traders is changing and higher prices can be expected. Conversely, a doji at a high point that is followed by a long black candle means that sentiment among traders is changing and lower prices can be expected. A tremendous variety of candlestick patterns can show a trader how the supply and demand picture is shaping up. We will examine these patterns in Chapters 3 and 4.

SUMMARY

Japanese candlestick charts have been around for hundreds of years but have gained in popularity in the Western world only over the last 20 years or so. Candlestick charts were designed to capture the mindset of traders as their actions can alter supply and demand dynamics, which in turn cause price movement. Candlestick charts have their roots in a militaristic culture that stressed planning, patience, discipline, and unwavering execution, all of which are valuable traits to modern traders. Of the most widely used charting options available to traders, candlestick charts provide the greatest depth of information. Combining the ancient methodology of candlestick charting with more modern methods in technical analysis can provide a synergy that will be examined in more detail in Chapters 5 through 8.

CHAPTER 2

Candlestick Construction and Analysis

Candlesticks are constructed by using the same data that are used for bar charts. The open, high, low, and close are all represented for the time period being plotted (intraday, daily, weekly, or monthly). Although each plot uses the same data, a candle plot provides much more insight into the psychology of traders, based not only on the candle shape but also on its color. This allows a deeper level of interpretation and analysis. Candlesticks place great emphasis on the relationship between the opening and closing prices each day. The implications of candlestick patterns are usually short-term in nature, but later we will use longer-term time frames along with trend analysis and price-based momentum indicators to find longer-term trading opportunities. This chapter will focus on the basic candlestick lines which are the foundation for the development of more complex interpretation and analysis. Figure 2-1 shows a comparison between a bar and a candlestick.

THE REAL BODY

The *real body* of a candlestick represents the range between the open and the close for the time period being plotted. A black (or filled) real body shows that the closing price was below the opening price for the period, signaling that the bears (or sellers) are in control. A white (or empty) candle shows that the closing price

FIGURE 2-1

Comparison between a Bar and a Candlestick

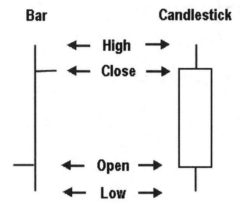

was above the opening price, signaling that the bulls (or buyers) are in control. It is the color and size of real bodies on a price chart that can give a trader instant feedback on whether the bulls or the bears are in control of a market or security along with their level of conviction. Long real bodies show strong conviction while short real bodies show indecision since the opening and closing prices for the period were not very far apart. Figure 2-2 shows the difference in the appearance of the real body depending on the open-close price relationship.

SHADOWS

Shadows, or *wicks* as they are sometimes called, are thin lines above and below the real body of a candle. Shadows represent price movement outside the real body during the time period. The shadow above the real body is called the *upper shadow*, and the shadow below the real body is called the *lower shadow*. The end points of the shadows represent the high of the period (upper shadow) and the low of the period (lower shadow). Typically, longer shadows with smaller real bodies represent periods of indecision among traders as price reached extremes during the period yet closed very near the open. Figure 2-3 shows shadows on candlesticks.

FIGURE 2-2

Real Bodies in White and Black Candles

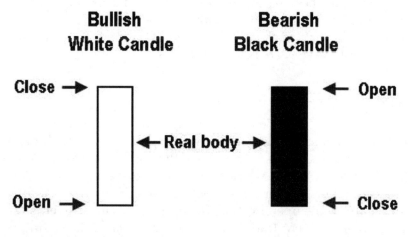

FIGURE 2-3

Candle Shadows

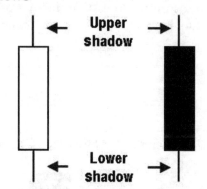

Shadows represent the upper and
lower extremes for the period.

BASIC CANDLESTICK LINES

Candlesticks are classified into categories on the basis of the size of the real body and shadows. This is one of the unique qualities of candlesticks that give them an edge over standard bar charts in analyzing price movement. Each classification has implications for who is in control of the market (bulls or bears) or whether there is indecision, which increases the odds of a reversal in price direction. Recognition of these basic candlestick lines is important because more complex patterns begin with these simple lines. If you are new to candlestick charting, take a few extra minutes to acquaint yourself with these very meaningful lines.

LONG CANDLES

A trading period in which the opening and closing values are far apart is known as a long candle or a long day. The length of the candle in this case refers to the size of the real body. These candles indicate strong price movement and are viewed as bullish (long white candle) or bearish (long black candle). How far is far apart with regard to the opening and closing prices? The answer is that it is relative to recent trading action over the last 5 to 10 trading periods. If the candle is noticeably longer than most of its predecessors within that time window, it is a valid signal that either buyers or sellers are assuming control of the market, depending on the color of the candle. Figure 2-4 shows long candles.

FIGURE 2-4

Long Candles

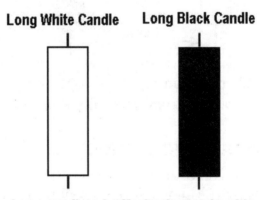

Long candles signify dominance by either
buyers or sellers, depending on the color.

FIGURE 2-5

Short Candles

The color of the candle is not as important as the close proximity of the opening and closing prices, especially in trending markets.

SHORT CANDLES

As I am sure you have figured out by now, short candles are candles in which the opening and closing prices are closer to each other relative to recent candles. The significance of short candles depends on where they appear. For example, short candles in a range-bound sideways market have much less meaning than they do if a short candle appears after a long uptrend or downtrend. Also, volume plays an important role in analyzing short candles. If a short candle appears in a trending market on heavier than normal volume, that is a sign that a change in price direction may be near as the bulls and the bears battle for control. The color of the candles is not as important as the close proximity of the opening and closing prices. Figure 2-5 shows short candles.

SHAVEN HEADS AND SHAVEN BOTTOMS, OR MARUBOZU

A candle that has no shadow at the top is referred to as a *shaven head,* and a candle that has no shadow at the bottom is referred to as a *shaven bottom.* The Japanese term for this is *marubozu,* which means "bald or shaven head."

A *white marubozu* is a long white candle that has no shadow at either end. This is considered bullish as it signifies that the open was at or very near the low of the period and the close was at or

FIGURE 2-6

Marubozu Lines

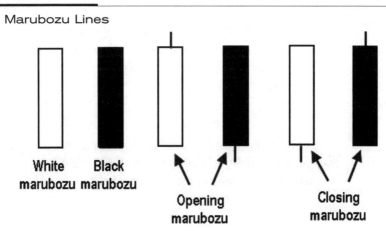

very near the high of the period. A *black marubozu* is a long black candle that has no shadow at either end. This is considered bearish as it signifies that the opening price was at or very near the high of the period and the closing price was at or very near the low of the period. A *closing marubozu* is a candle that has no shadow at the closing end of the body, and an *opening marubozu* is a candle that has no shadow at the opening end of the body. Figure 2-6 shows marubozu lines.

SPINNING TOP

A *spinning top* is a candle that has a small or short real body with shadows at each end. Some believe that a spinning top needs shadows that are each longer than the real body, whereas others believe that the length of the shadows is irrelevant. I subscribe to the latter interpretation as in my opinion the small real body is evidence enough of trader indecision as the bulls and the bears struggle to dictate price direction. The upper and lower shadows show that both the bulls and the bears were exerting pressure during the period but in the end price closed near the open. Remember that as with all short candles, the color is not as

FIGURE 2-7

Spinning Tops

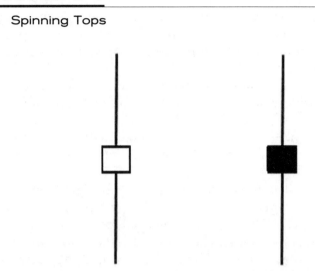

important as what the candle signifies. Spinning tops have much more importance when they appear in a trending market, especially on an increase in volume. Figure 2-7 shows spinning tops.

DOJI

A *doji* forms when a candle's opening and closing prices are virtually equal. This is another candle line that shows indecision among traders and signifies a possible reversal in price direction.

A doji derives its importance from the context in which it appears. Just like a spinning top, its formation is much more significant in a trending market than in a range-bound choppy market. Also, a doji gains more importance if recent price action has not produced many doji. Basically, the more doji there are, the less important they are. A doji that forms in a trending market means that a trend change is a possibility as the mindset of traders (as reflected by price movement) has reached a point of indecision. Just as the psychology of uptrends (more sanguine) is different from the psychology of downtrends (more fearful), so too is the predictive ability of doji in these market environments.

The appearance of a doji in an uptrend more than likely signifies that the buying power necessary to continue the uptrend may be waning. A doji in a downtrend can be less reliable since price sometimes can continue to fall simply because there is not enough buying pressure to reverse the trend. Figure 2-8 shows a doji.

Although a doji is known for the very close proximity of its opening and closing prices, there are also doji that have unique names and provide extra insight into trader psychology. The location of the opening and closing prices along with the existence of and length of the shadows can help a trader identify specific doji lines.

A *long-legged doji* is considered a reversal signal when it appears in a trending market. True to the doji pattern, it has a very narrow real body, typically appearing as what looks like a dash at or near the center of the candle. The shadows of the candle are very long in relation to the narrow real body. A long-legged doji demonstrates a battle for control between buyers and sellers throughout the day. Although each side had periods in which it looked to be winning the battle, neither was able to sustain consistent pressure to move the price either up or down, as demonstrated by the close proximity of the opening and closing prices. Figure 2-9 shows a long-legged doji.

The *gravestone doji* shown in Figure 2-10 is a bearish candle that shows the opening and closing prices at the bottom of the price

FIGURE 2-8

Doji

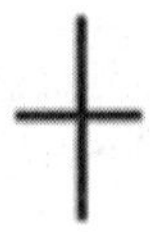

A doji shows indecision among traders as the open and close for the period are very close, if not identical.

FIGURE 2-9

Long-Legged Doji

A long-legged doji shows a battle over price direction that ends in a stalemate for the period.

FIGURE 2-10

Gravestone Doji

A gravestone doji is bearish as it shows the inability of buyers to sustain an upward price movement.

range for the period. Its name is derived from soldiers (late buyers) dying in battle, which equates to the end of an uptrend. This particular doji shows that after trading opened, price was pushed noticeably higher, only to reverse lower and close at or near the opening price of the period. This demonstrates a failure of buyers to be able to sustain upward price movement. This is particularly

FIGURE 2-11

Dragonfly Doji

**A dragonfly doji is bullish in downtrends as it shows the
inability of sellers to sustain a downward price movement.**

bearish in an uptrending market and points to the strong possibility of a reversal lower in price. The longer the upper shadow, the
more bearish its implications.

A *dragonfly doji* is the opposite of a gravestone doji. It is
formed when the opening and closing prices are at or near the
high of the period. This candle shows that sellers had things going
their way during the period but were unable to maintain control as
price reversed and closed back where it opened. This is extremely
bullish behavior in a downtrending market as dragonfly doji often
mark important reversal points in downtrends. Two patterns that
are related to the dragonfly doji are the *hammer* and the *hanging
man,* which will be discussed in Chapter 3. The longer the lower
shadow is, the more bullish the implications of the dragonfly doji
are. Figure 2-11 shows a dragonfly doji.

STARS

A *star* is a candle that forms in a trending market. Its presence can
indicate that the prevailing trend is in danger of reversing. Star
reversal patterns consist of multiple candles and are classified into
four varieties. Their interpretation and implications are covered in
more detail in Chapter 3.

A star consists of a candle with a small real body (most likely a
spinning top or doji) that gaps away from the previous candle in a

FIGURE 2-12

Stars

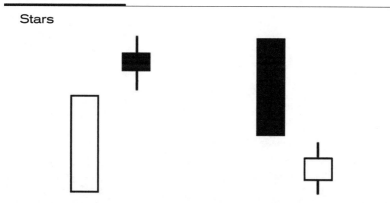

The formation of a star in a trending market is a sign that the prevailing trend may be in danger of reversing.

trending market. The real body of the star should not overlap with the previous candle. The color of the candle that forms the star is not important because its significance is derived from the virtual stalemate for the period between buyers and sellers. For a candle to be classified as a star, there must be a trend in place to potentially reverse. To be a valid star in an uptrending market, the star should form after a long white candle, whereas in a downtrend a star should form after a long black candle. Figure 2-12 shows basic examples of stars.

SUMMARY

Candlestick charts use the same data as bar charts (open, high, low, and close) but provide additional insights into the mindset of traders. The color and size of the real body indicate whether buyers or sellers are in control of the market or security being traded or if there is indecision among traders. Shadows also show the high and low price extremes for the period being plotted. Candles with small real bodies such as doji, spinning tops, and stars show trader indecision and can have reversal implications if they appear in a trending market.

Candlestick
Reversal Patterns

Now that we have covered the basics of candlestick construction
along with some of the more important candle lines, it is time to
look at reversal patterns. One of the major advantages of candlestick charting is its ability to show changes in trader sentiment at
key turning points in the market. These changes in sentiment are
reflected by *reversal patterns*. A reversal pattern consists of groups
of candles that show a shift in market psychology that can alert an
astute trader that a change in price direction may be near. Being
able to identify these patterns can help a trader get an earlier jump
on a change in price trend than may be possible with other charting
methodologies.

Many documented candlestick reversal patterns have been
discovered over the years, but the purpose and scope of this
chapter is to acquaint you with the most common, useful patterns.
A brief discussion, chart examples, and trading notes (support,
resistance, and stop placement) will be given for each pattern
listed in this chapter. Actual trading off some of these patterns will
be discussed in more detail in Chapter 8. The end of this chapter
will examine some reversal patterns that tend to mark longer-term
price reversals in the market.

UMBRELLA LINES

Umbrella lines are candles that have their real bodies (opening and closing prices) near the high of the day. They also have long shadows, or tails, that signify that sellers were active during the period. An umbrella line should have a very small, if any, upper shadow. The color of the real body is not important. Umbrella lines draw their significance from the context in which they appear. For example, an umbrella line in a sideways or range-bound market is insignificant, whereas an umbrella line that appears in either an uptrending or a downtrending market is an early sign of a potential price reversal. Umbrella lines come in two types: *hammer* and *hanging man*. Figure 3-1 shows that even though the formations of the hammer and the hanging man are the same, they have different meanings, depending on market conditions.

A *hammer* appears in a downtrend and is an early indication of a potential bottom. It is called a hammer because its shape resembles that of a hammer. The candle opens the period at or near its high for that period. As trading progresses, sellers push the price lower in what looks to be a continuation of the downtrend. During the period, however, buyers step in and push the price back until it is close to the opening price. This is a clear win for the

FIGURE 3-1

Hammer or Hanging Man

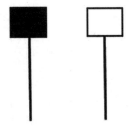

The hammer and the hanging man look the same. Their names and meaning are derived from the context in which they appear. The real body color is not important.

bulls and shows that buyers are digging in their heels because they see value at the price level at which the hammer appears.

Figure 3-2, a daily chart of the Nasdaq Composite Index, shows how hammers appear in downtrending markets. Remember, for a hammer to be a valid reversal signal, there must be downward movement to reverse. If a hammer appears in a sideways or range-bound market, it should be viewed as insignificant. A hammer usually precedes a reversal higher in price, but the hammer itself has no forecasting value in terms of how far or for how long price will move higher once it reverses. Note the small upper shadows on each hammer as the hammers formed on June 8 and July 1, 2010. Since the psychology of downtrends is based more on fear, reversals off hammers are not always instantaneous as it may take some time for buyers to gain enough confidence to wade back into the market. Nevertheless, their appearance is a bullish sign that shows that the market is trying to "hammer out" a bottom.

FIGURE 3-2

Two Hammers: Nasdaq Composite Index, Daily

Source: MetaStock

A *hanging man* is formed the same way as a hammer, but its meaning comes from the fact that it is formed after the market has been trending higher. This line gets its name because when it appears in an uptrend, it looks like a man hanging with his legs dangling. A hanging man forms when price opens for the period and then moves lower as traders take profits, after which the price closes back up into the vicinity of where it opened. After all this energy expended climbing back up near the opening price, there is very little gain, if any, to show for the period. This is a bearish sign that sellers are increasing their activity. An example of a hanging man is shown in the daily chart of the NYSE Composite Index in Figure 3-3. Notice how the appearance of the hanging man on November 8 was an indication that price was ready to reverse lower. Since a sense of complacency can set in for markets that are in an uptrend, a hanging man usually requires some form of confirmation that a price reversal is indeed developing. The long black

FIGURE 3-3

Hanging Man: NYSE Composite Index, Daily

Source: MetaStock

candle on November 9 provided confirmation that selling pressure was increasing.

The hammer and the hanging man provide a deeper insight into the psychology of the market. Understanding this psychology is paramount to identifying and profiting from these patterns. Their appearance can be summed up by the following points:

- First and foremost there must be a trend to reverse to give these lines significance.
- Their formation shows that sellers were active (long lower shadow) during the period but price closed very near where it opened.
- This is bullish behavior in a downtrend (hammer) but bearish behavior in an uptrend (hanging man).
- Reversals off hammers may take slightly longer as the market tries to hammer out a bottom.
- It is always wise to wait for some form of confirmation before declaring a reversal in either case.

When one is trading a hammer pattern, a stop should be placed just below the low of the lower shadow or tail. For that reason, it is best to wait for some sort of price pullback to "test" the low formed on the hammer candle to reduce risk exposure (the distance between your buy price and the stop).

When one is trading a hanging man, it is best to wait for confirmation of a reversal before a short position is entered. Confirmation can be in the form of a close below the real body of the hanging man. The stop should be placed above the high of the hanging man.

ENGULFING PATTERNS

An engulfing pattern forms when the real body of a candle fully engulfs the real body of the previous candle that is the opposite color. Just like umbrella lines, these patterns gain their meaning from the context in which they appear. A *bullish engulfing pattern* consists of a large white candle whose real body engulfs the real body of a black candle in a downtrend. A *bearish engulfing pattern* consists of a large black candle whose body engulfs the real body of a white candle in an uptrend.

Although only an engulfing of the real body is necessary to create a valid engulfing pattern, the more of the previous candle that is engulfed (including shadows), the stronger the signal. The appearance of a bearish engulfing pattern in an upward-trending market increases the possibility that all those who wanted to buy during the uptrend may have done so already, with the final gap up on the engulfing day seen as the last-gasp push higher. The same logic applies to the market psychology behind a bullish engulfing pattern in a downtrend as buyers step in to reverse the price higher. Engulfing patterns have little or no meaning in a sideways, choppy market. Figure 3-4 shows engulfing patterns.

The psychology of an engulfing pattern in a trending market actually screams reversal as price opens for the period by gapping in the direction of the trend before reversing to close strongly against the prevailing trend. A bearish engulfing pattern starts out in a very bullish mindset for traders since a gap higher (a *rising window*) shows strong bullish sentiment. The price reversal shows

FIGURE 3-4

Engulfing Patterns

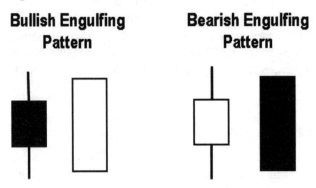

Bullish Engulfing Pattern

Bearish Engulfing Pattern

Whether the candles have tails or shadows is irrelevant. An engulfing pattern is measured only by the length of the real bodies.

a "turning of the tide" as traders reconsider their positions, demonstrated by a pronounced selling of shares. The daily chart of Google in Figure 3-5 shows an example of a bearish engulfing pattern. Note the following sequence that reveals the market psychology behind this pattern:

1. Google had been moving higher since late 2006 (the very left side of the chart).
2. After a brief pullback, price pushed higher in an attempt to continue the uptrend.
3. On February 1, 2007, price gapped higher, opening above the entire range of the previous day before sellers emerged to drive price lower. This action created a black candle that engulfed the previous day's white candle.

The behavior at this reversal point shows that the positive sentiment shown by the bulls at the open on February 1, 2007,

FIGURE 3-5

Bearish Engulfing Pattern for Google, Daily

Source: MetaStock

dissipated rather quickly, which resulted in a failure at the previous high at around 510. This was a bearish sign that showed strong selling pressure in the 510 area that led to a change in price trend.

The mindset behind a bullish engulfing pattern is the same, except in the other direction. The pattern starts with a gap lower (*falling window*), which shows strong bearish sentiment. Buyers then step in and buy shares, which causes price to reverse high enough to engulf the previous black candle. Figure 3-6 shows a daily chart of the Nasdaq Composite Index that has an interesting combination of candles in May 2009. Note how two spinning tops formed on May 21 and 22 after a brief pullback. The next trading day (May 26), a bullish engulfing pattern was formed that showed that buyers were ready to take the market higher. The bullish engulfing pattern actually engulfed the real bodies of *three* previous black candles. This sent a very powerful signal that the pullback was weak as traders were indecisive (two spinning

FIGURE 3-6

Bullish Engulfing Pattern: Nasdaq Composite, Daily

Source: MetaStock

tops) followed by a powerful move higher as buyers stepped in to complete the bullish engulfing pattern.

Engulfing patterns are very powerful signals that a change in price direction is due. Their appearance in trending markets shows that sentiment is changing as price gaps open in the direction of the trend and close in the opposite direction. Remember that engulfing patterns have meaning in a trending market. Engulfing patterns that appear in choppy, sloppy markets are best ignored.

When one is trading engulfing patterns, stops are placed just above or below the extreme price between the two candles that form the engulfing pattern. In a bullish engulfing pattern, support is at the lowest point of the two candles that formed the engulfing pattern. The stop should be placed just below that support level. In a bearish engulfing pattern, resistance is at the highest point of the two candles that formed the engulfing pattern. The stop should be placed just above that resistance level.

DARK CLOUD COVER

A *dark cloud cover* is a bearish reversal pattern that occurs in an uptrend. Just as dark clouds warn of an approaching storm, this two-candle pattern shows a negative change in market sentiment. Figure 3-7 shows a dark cloud cover.

FIGURE 3-7

Dark Cloud Cover

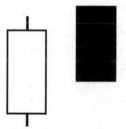

The open of the second candle opens over the HIGH of the white candle and then reverses and closes at least halfway into the white candle's real body

The formation of the pattern begins with a long white candle in an established uptrend. The next candle opens *over the high* of the white candle. This is a very important point. Although most comparisons in candle patterns are between real bodies, this open must be above the previous candles' actual high (the top of the upper shadow if one is present). The dark cloud cover is recognized as follows:

1. Price must be in an uptrend.
2. After a long white candle, price gaps higher, opening above the *high* of the white candle.
3. Price reverses lower and closes at least halfway (preferably more) into the real body of the white candle.

This pattern shows a shift in sentiment as the gap open in the direction of the trend lacks sufficient buying support to continue the trend. Since the reversal is strong enough to wipe out over half of the previous candle's gains, it gives bullish traders pause and causes them to rethink their commitment to the security being traded. The deeper the penetration into the white candle's real body, the greater the chance of a top. Resistance is at the top of the black candle in this formation. The daily chart of Citigroup in Figure 3-8 shows a dark cloud cover.

The dark cloud cover has even more significance if the open of the second candle gaps over an existing key resistance level and then reverses lower. This behavior shows failure at a point where price had turned lower at least once before. Resistance areas are covered in more detail in Chapter 5.

It is also possible for the second candle to reverse and close completely below the previous day's white candle, forming a bearish engulfing pattern. Remember, the deeper the sell-off on the second candle, the more bearish its implications. When one is trading a dark cloud cover, resistance is the high point of the second candle of the dark cloud cover pattern. A stop should be placed just above that level.

PIERCING LINE

The *piercing line* pattern is the bullish counterpart to the dark cloud cover. This two-candle pattern occurs in downtrends. The pattern begins with a long black candle. The next candle opens below the

FIGURE 3-8

Dark Cloud Cover for Citigroup, Daily

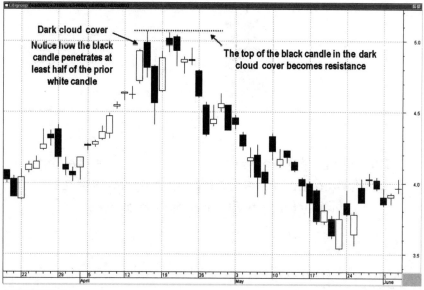

Source: MetaStock

low of the black candle. Again, it is important to note that the open must be below the *low* of the black candle, which means below the bottom of the lower shadow (if a lower shadow exists). To be considered a piercing line, the candle must reverse and close at least halfway into the real body of the previous black candle. Figure 3-9 shows a piercing line.

A piercing line is shown in Figure 3-10, a daily chart of IBM. The piercing line is recognized as follows:

1. Price must be in a downtrend.
2. After a long black candle, price gaps lower, opening below the *low* of the black candle.
3. Price reverses higher and closes at least halfway (preferably more) into the real body of the black candle.

The piercing line pattern that was completed on July 1, 2008, preceded a sharp rally for the remainder of the month. The low of the piercing line pattern becomes a support level since that is the price level at which buyers became active enough to reverse price direction.

FIGURE 3-9

Piercing Line

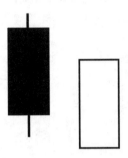

The second candle opens below the LOW of the first candle and then reverses higher and closes at least halfway into the first candle's real body.

FIGURE 3-10

Piercing Line Pattern for IBM, Daily

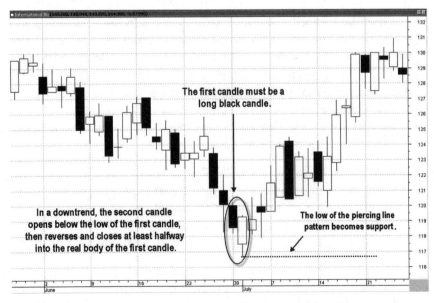

The first candle must be a long black candle.

In a downtrend, the second candle opens below the low of the first candle, then reverses and closes at least halfway into the real body of the first candle.

The low of the piercing line pattern becomes support.

Source: MetaStock

It is very important to verify that the second candle closes at least halfway into the real body of the first candle to show sufficient conviction among buyers for a reversal in trend. If the second candle falls short of the halfway point, further confirmation is needed, such as a higher close on the subsequent candle. Otherwise, the odds increase for a continuation of the downtrend.

When one is trading a piercing line pattern, support is at the low of the second candle in the piercing line pattern. A stop should be placed just beneath that low.

STARS

The identification and classification of stars was discussed in Chapter 2; now we will examine their reversal implications. A star is composed of a small real body that has gapped above a long real body in an uptrend or below a long real body in a downtrend. There should be no overlap of real bodies between the two candles. Think of a star as a spinning top or doji that gaps away from a long body candle in the direction of the prevailing trend. The color of the real body of the star is not important. The appearance of the star represents a struggle between buyers and sellers that puts the continuation of the existing trend in doubt. Stars come in four types:

1. Morning star
2. Evening star
3. Doji star
4. Shooting star

Morning Star

As its name implies, a *morning star* is a sign of hope, or a sunrise to begin a new day. The appearance of a morning star gives hope that a downtrend is losing steam and may be ready to reverse. This pattern consists of a spinning top or doji that is between two long real bodies. Figure 3-11 shows a morning star pattern. The pattern is formed as follows:

1. A long black candle is formed that shows that the bears are in control.

FIGURE 3-11

Morning Star Pattern

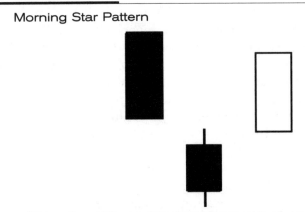

The color of the real body of the real body on the second candle is unimportant.

2. The second candle gaps away from the long black candle, with no overlap between their real bodies. This shows that the sellers started strong but could not sustain their early momentum. The color of the real body of the second candle is unimportant.
3. The third candle is a white candle that penetrates the real body of the first candle, showing that buyers are assuming control. This candle is even more bullish if it gaps away from the second candle. The deeper the penetration into the black candle, the more bullish the reversal signal. An increase in volume on the third candle also helps confirm the reversal.

The daily chart of Citigroup in Figure 3-12 shows a morning star pattern. Notice how the second candle gaps away from the first in the downtrend. The third candle then gaps higher and penetrates deep into the body of the first candle of the pattern, forming a bullish reversal.

Since the morning star is a three-candle pattern, it is best to wait for the completion of the third candle before initiating a long trade. When one is trading a morning star pattern, the low of the

FIGURE 3-12

Morning Star Pattern for Citigroup, Daily

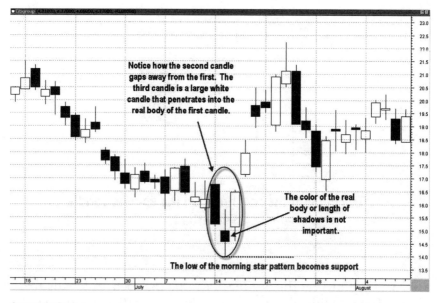

Notice how the second candle gaps away from the first. The third candle is a large white candle that penetrates into the real body of the first candle.

The color of the real body or length of shadows is not important.

The low of the morning star pattern becomes support

Source: MetaStock

second candle of the pattern is support. A protective stop loss should be placed just below that level.

Evening Star

An *evening star* is a bearish reversal pattern that is the opposite of a morning star. Figure 3-13 shows an evening star pattern. The evening star pattern appears in an uptrend and is formed as follows:

1. A long white candle is formed that shows that the bulls are in control.
2. The second candle gaps away from the long white candle, with no overlap between their real bodies. This shows that the buyers started strong but could not sustain their early momentum. The color of the real body of the second candle is unimportant.

FIGURE 3-13

Evening Star Pattern

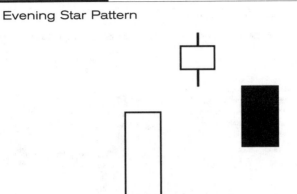

**The color of the real body on the second candle is
unimportant.**

3. The third candle is a black candle that penetrates the real
   body of the first candle, showing that sellers are assuming
   control. This candle is even more bearish if it gaps away
   from the second candle. The deeper the penetration into
   the white candle, the more bearish the reversal signal. An
   increase in volume on the third candle also helps confirm
   the reversal.

The daily chart of NVIDIA Corporation in Figure 3-14 shows
an evening star pattern. Note how price gapped higher after the
long white candle in an uptrend.

Just as with the morning star pattern, it is best to wait for the
completion of the third candle before initiating a short trade. When
one is initiating a short position on the evening star pattern, the
high of the second candle of the pattern is resistance. A protective
stop loss should be placed just above that level.

Doji Star

A *doji star* is also a three-candle pattern that is identical in all
respects to the morning and evening star patterns just discussed

FIGURE 3-14

Evening Star Pattern for NVIDIA Corporation, Daily

The second candle gaps away from the first. The third candle is a black candle that penetrates into the real body of the first candle.

Source: MetaStock

except that the second candle of the pattern must be a doji. A pronounced gap in the direction of the reversal gives the pattern a higher degree of reliability. An increase in volume on the reversal (third) candle also gives the pattern more credibility. Figure 3-15 shows doji star patterns.

If there is complete separation between each candle in the sequence (i.e., no overlap of any kind), these are referred to in Western technical analysis as island reversals. In Japanese candlestick terminology, they are called *abandoned babies*. A morning doji star that is completely separated from the other two candles by gaps (no overlap) is referred to as an *abandoned baby bottom,* and an evening doji star that is completely separated from the other two candles by gaps is called an *abandoned baby top.* These patterns can be *invalidated* if the third candle is the same color and is moving in the same direction as the first candle of the formation. For example, an evening doji star is invalidated if the third candle is white and closes above the real body of the doji candle. It is always important

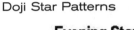

FIGURE 3-15

Doji Star Patterns

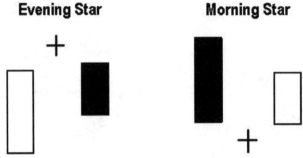

The key to the doji star pattern is the gap between the real bodies between the first and second candles.

to let the pattern develop instead of jumping into a trade early by assuming that the third candle will automatically complete the reversal. This will help prevent needless losses.

The daily chart of Google in Figure 3-16 shows an evening doji star. Note that the second candle is a doji that gapped away from the long white candle on July 21, 2005. The third candle is black, but the real body is not what would necessarily be considered a long candle; however, the gap lower on the third candle shows strong conviction among sellers just the same.

When one is trading the doji star patterns, stops should be placed just above or below the second candle of the pattern. For example, when one is short selling the evening star pattern, a protective stop should be placed just above the high of the doji, which represents meaningful resistance. When one is buying the morning star pattern, a protective stop should be placed just under the low of the doji, which represents meaningful support.

Shooting Star or Inverted Hammer

A *shooting star* consists of a small real body at the bottom of its range for the period with a long upper shadow. This pattern is bearish in uptrends as it shows that buyers kept the uptrend going for part of the period but sellers knocked the closing price back

FIGURE 3-16

Evening Doji Star Pattern for Google, Daily

The second candle is a doji that shows trader uncertainty and warns of a reversal.

The high of the doji star becomes resistance.

The gap between the doji and the third candle shows strong trader conviction.

Source: MetaStock

down close to or equal to the opening price. The color of the real body is unimportant. If the closing price is the same as or very close to the opening price to give the appearance of no real body, this will create a gravestone doji (see Chapter 2), which is more bearish than a shooting star. The shooting star consists of a single candle that requires some form of confirmation to validate a price reversal. Typically, this confirmation comes from a close below the real body of the shooting star that shows that sellers are assuming control of the price action. Figure 3-17 shows a shooting star.

Shooting stars reveal resistance areas as price gaps to the upside and moves higher, but sellers emerge to push the closing price back down to near the opening price, leaving a long upper shadow. The daily chart of Intel Corp. (INTC) in Figure 3-18 shows a shooting star that formed in August 2009. In this case the shooting star signaled a pause in the uptrend as the price began a month-long consolidation period.

An *inverted hammer* has the same appearance as a shooting star except that it appears in a downtrend and is a signal that a

FIGURE 3-17

Shooting Star

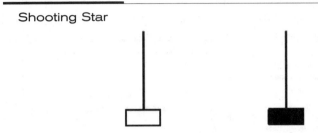

A shooting star consists of a small real body and a long upper shadow. The color of the real body is unimportant.

FIGURE 3-18

Shooting Star, Intel Corp., Daily

Source: MetaStock

price reversal higher may be imminent. As with a shooting star, the color of the real body on an inverted hammer is unimportant. The psychology behind the inverted hammer is interesting in that its appearance often emboldens short sellers to initiate new short positions because it gives the impression of real weakness among buyers as their effort to push price higher has failed. Price sometimes will continue lower early in the next session before reversing higher. The price reversal itself often is fueled by short covering as new, late-to-the-party short players begin to see their positions move against them. Confirmation of a price reversal comes with a close over the real body of the inverted hammer. The daily chart of IBM in Figure 3-19 shows an inverted hammer. Notice how price opened the next day and began moving lower, which emboldened new short sellers. By the end of that day, however, a hammer formed as late shorts were forced to cover; that drove the reversal higher.

FIGURE 3-19

Inverted Hammer for IBM, Daily

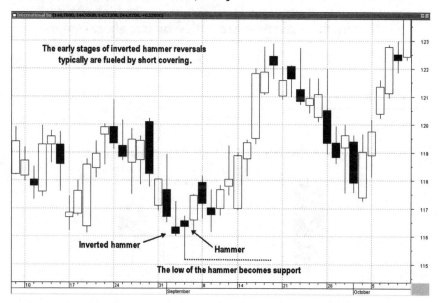

Source: MetaStock

HARAMI

A *harami* is similar to the inside day in Western technical analysis. The only difference is that the inside day requires the *entire* second bar to be inside the first, whereas the harami involves only the *real bodies* of the candles. A harami is a two-candle pattern that occurs in a trending market and can be thought of as a reverse engulfing pattern. In a harami pattern, the first candle is a long white candle in an uptrend or a long black candle in a downtrend. In most cases the color of the second real body is opposite the color of the first, but that is not necessary to form a valid harami pattern. The term *harami* means "pregnant" in Japanese, with the first longer candle representing the "mother" and the second, contained candle representing the "baby." Figure 3-20 shows bullish and bearish harami patterns.

A *bullish harami* is formed when:

1. The market is in an established downtrend.
2. A long black candle is formed, showing that sellers are in control.
3. The next candle begins with a gap higher open (rising window) as previous short sellers cover their positions. Any further advances are muted by late short traders

FIGURE 3-20

Harami

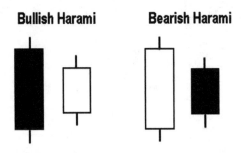

Bullish Harami   **Bearish Harami**

The real body of the second candle must be within the real body of the first.

jumping in to catch the next push lower, which causes the real body of the second candle to remain inside the first.

4. A close above the high of the first candle is needed to confirm the reversal.

A *bearish harami* is formed when:

1. The market is in an established uptrend.

2. A long white candle is formed, showing that buyers are in control.

3. The next candle begins with a gap lower open (falling window) as previous buyers take profits. Any further declines are muted by late buyers jumping in to catch the next push higher, which causes the real body of the second candle to remain inside the first.

A close below the low of the first candle is needed to confirm the reversal.

The daily chart of the Nasdaq Composite Index in Figure 3-21 shows a bullish harami.

FIGURE 3-21

Bullish Harami for Nasdaq Composite, Daily

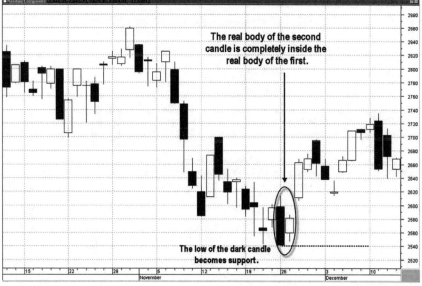

The real body of the second candle is completely inside the real body of the first.

The low of the dark candle becomes support.

Source: MetaStock

HARAMI CROSS

The *harami cross* is an even stronger reversal pattern because the second, or inside, candle is a doji. Typically, the smaller the real body of the second candle, the stronger the signal as it shows a real battle going on for near-term direction in the face of the prevailing trend. The daily chart of Amazon.com in Figure 3-22 shows a bearish harami cross. Note how the first candle on August 11, 2008, had a long upper shadow that demonstrated strong selling pressure at the upper end of the range. The harami cross was followed immediately by a spinning top that showed a continuing struggle for short-term direction of the market. The price of Amazon eventually dropped to the low 40s by late October.

TWEEZER TOPS AND BOTTOMS

Tweezer tops and *tweezer bottoms* are two or more candle lines with either matching highs or matching lows. These patterns get their

FIGURE 3-22

Bearish Harami Cross for Amazon.com Inc., Daily

Source: MetaStock

names because the matching tops or bottoms tend to look like a pair of tweezers. The ideal tweezer pattern consists of a long first candle followed by a second candle with a small real body that shows a loss of momentum in the direction of the trend. Tweezer patterns take on a higher level of significance if they occur at established support or resistance levels. They are also more meaningful on longer-term charts such as weekly or monthly.

In an uptrending market, a tweezer top is formed when two or more highs are the same. In a downtrend, a tweezer bottom is formed when two or more lows are the same. The candles forming the tweezer pattern do not necessarily have to be consecutive candles. Tweezer patterns are also more powerful when the combination of equal highs or equal lows comes in the form of a reversal pattern itself, such as an engulfing pattern or a harami cross. More weight is given if the second candle is a hammer, hanging man, spinning top, or doji. The color of the candles is not important. Figure 3-23 shows tweezer patterns.

The daily chart of F5 Networks Inc. in Figure 3-24 shows an example of a tweezer top. Note that the first candle is a white candle followed by a small-bodied black candle. The second candle in the tweezer pattern was a spinning top, which increased the odds for a

FIGURE 3-23

Tweezer Top and Tweezer Bottom

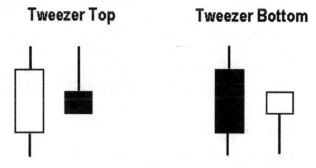

Tweezer Top   Tweezer Bottom

The combination or color of candles is not important as a tweezer top or bottom is formed by consecutive highs (top) or lows (bottom)

FIGURE 3-24

Tweezer Top for F5 Networks Inc., Daily

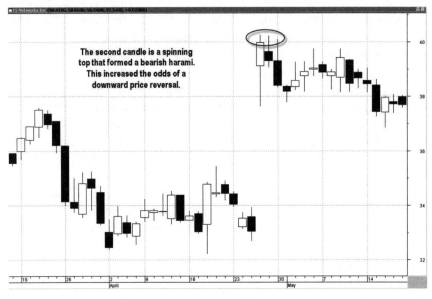

The second candle is a spinning top that formed a bearish harami. This increased the odds of a downward price reversal.

Source: MetaStock

price reversal. The reversal was confirmed by a long black candle, which showed that sellers were increasing their activity.

When one is trading the tweezer pattern, it is best to wait for confirmation in the form of a higher close over the first candle of the formation in a tweezer bottom or a close under the first long candle in a tweezer top. Resistance on a tweezer top is at the matching highs, which means a stop should be placed just above that level. Support on a tweezer bottom is at the matching lows, which means that a stop should be placed just below that level.

BELT HOLD LINES

A *belt hold line* is a long candle line that appears in a trending market and is the opposite color of the trend (a white candle in a downtrend or a black candle in an uptrend). This candle line should be an opening marubozu (open at the extreme high or low for the period), but a small shadow past the opening extreme is acceptable.

FIGURE 3-25

Bullish Belt Hold and Bearish Belt Hold

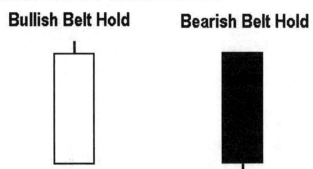

Bullish Belt Hold   Bearish Belt Hold

Belt Hold Lines warn of a possible price reversal as price opens in the direction of the trend but then reverses against the trend.

A *bullish belt hold* appears in a downtrend. It is a long white candle that opens at the low (or very near the low) of the period and closes at or near the high for the period. The bullish belt hold candle has more importance if there have been relatively few on the chart before its formation. A *bearish belt hold* appears in an uptrend. It is a long black candle that opens at or very near its high for the period and closes at or near its low for the period. The bearish belt hold also gains more importance if it follows a period of smaller real body candles. Figure 3-25 shows belt hold lines.

The daily chart of the iShares Russell 2000 Index Fund ETF (exchange-traded fund) in Figure 3-26 shows both bullish and bearish belt hold lines. These lines are great for showing a potential change in price direction as their color is opposite that of the prevailing trend. Note in each case how their appearance preceded a short-term change in price direction.

Belt hold lines also can be a part of other, stronger reversal patterns such as piercing lines, dark cloud covers, and engulfing patterns. Using belt hold lines on their own to make trades (belt hold lines that are not part of other, more reliable reversal patterns) is not recommended. If you choose to do so, however, stops should be placed above the high (bearish belt hold) or below the low (bullish belt hold) of the belt hold line, depending on the trend.

FIGURE 3-26

Belt Hold Lines for iShares Russell 2000 Index Fund ETF, Daily

Source: MetaStock

THREE BLACK CROWS

Three black crows is a rare but ominous pattern that appears as an uptrend matures, warning of a pending price reversal. This pattern starts with a black candle opening near its high and closing near its low for the period. The next two candles should open within the real body of the previous candle (a small gap higher) before succumbing to selling pressure and closing at or near its low for the period. This pattern shows that the bulls are starting to trade in their direction before sellers take control and force a negative close near the low of the session. This signifies increasing strength of conviction among sellers. The three black crows pattern typically has longer-term implications in terms of price reversal. Figure 3-27 shows a three black crows pattern.

The daily chart of JPMorgan Chase in Figure 3-28 shows a three black crows pattern. In this case, the pattern is a variation

FIGURE 3-27

Three Black Crows Pattern

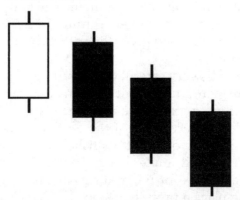

Each candle gaps into the real body of the previous candle and closes at or near the low of the period.

FIGURE 3-28

Three Black Crows for JPMorgan Chase, Daily

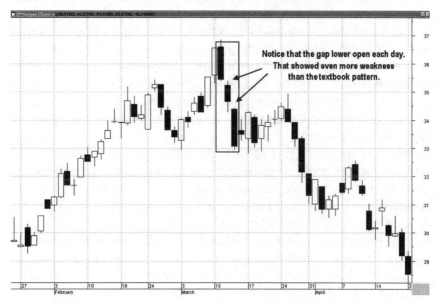

Source: MetaStock

of the "textbook" description of each subsequent candle opening within the real body of the previous candle. Notice how each candle actually gaps *down*, away from the real body of the previous candle, and never really recovers during the session. This shows pronounced weakness and gives the pattern more validity in forecasting lower prices.

One should be very careful when trading this pattern because upon its completion, a trader can be in an unfavorable risk position in terms of setting a stop since resistance is way back at the top of the three-day pattern. Also, if the decline is too large over the course of the three candles, bottom fishers may come in and begin nibbling, which could ignite a snap-back rally. It is best to wait for a bounce and look for the next reversal pattern to get a better opportunity to place a protective stop.

THREE WHITE SOLDIERS

The *three white soldiers* pattern is the opposite of the three black crows pattern in that it signifies price strength after a downtrend or a period of price consolidation. This pattern consists of three white candlesticks closing progressively higher and gives the appearance of steadily marching higher in the manner of advancing soldiers. The name *three white soldiers* is yet another military reference that reflects the culture back in Honma's day.

Each day should open within the body of the previous candle, and each close should be at or near each candle's high. This pattern shows that sellers are starting each day's trade in their direction before buyers overwhelm them and force a positive close near the high of the session, signifying increasing strength of conviction among buyers. Since this pattern gives the appearance of a steady advance, each candle needs to be long but not too long; otherwise, the pattern would give the appearance of moving too far too fast which could induce profit taking or attract aggressive short sellers. Also, if the pattern shows shorter candles as it progresses, that is a sign of weakness or less conviction among buyers and makes the pattern suspect. Figure 3-29 shows a three white soldiers pattern.

Figure 3-30 shows a three white soldiers pattern on the NYSE Composite Index as it comes off a low in March 2001. Notice how

FIGURE 3-29

Three White Soldiers Pattern

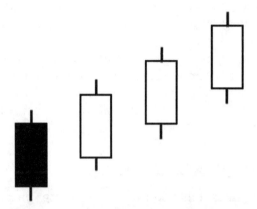

Each candle gaps into the real body of the previous candle and closes at or near the high of the period.

FIGURE 3-30

Three White Soldiers in NYSE Composite Index, Daily

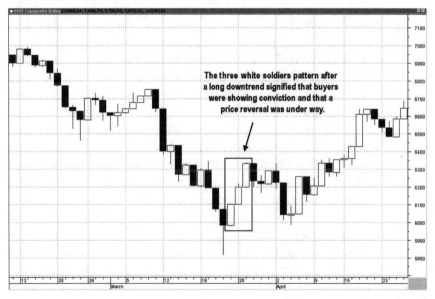

The three white soldiers pattern after a long downtrend signified that buyers were showing conviction and that a price reversal was under way.

Source: MetaStock

the pattern showed conviction among buyers and led to a change in price direction.

Trading this pattern requires care just as in the case with the three black crows pattern. Upon its completion, a trader can be in an unfavorable risk position in terms of setting a stop since support is at the bottom of the three-day pattern. Also, if the advance is too large over the course of the three candles, profit takers could emerge, which would cause the rally to lose upside momentum. It is best to wait for a pullback and look for the next reversal pattern to have a better opportunity to place a protective stop.

COUNTERATTACK LINES

Counterattack lines (also known as meeting lines) are formed when two opposite-colored candles close at virtually the same price level. This pattern can be thought of in military terms. For example, in a *bullish counterattack line*, the bears have their way in the first candle, forcing a lower close. The next candle's opening price gaps to the downside before the bulls rally and mount a counterattack, resulting in no change in the closing price from one candle to the next. A *bearish counterattack line* is just the opposite, as the bulls make an impressive showing on the first candle and the opening of the second, only to have the bears launch their counter-attack and force a stalemate with regard to the closing price from one candle to the next. Figure 3-31 shows counterattack lines.

Note that each of these patterns begins like the reversal patterns discussed earlier in this chapter. The bullish counter-attack line resembles the bullish piercing line, but price does not penetrate the real body at the close. The bearish counterattack line resembles the dark cloud cover, but it also does not penetrate the real body of the first candle on a closing basis. The lack of pene-tration of the previous candle's real body on a closing basis makes these lines less powerful than a piercing line or dark cloud cover.

The daily chart of the SPDR S&P Retail ETF in Figure 3-32 shows a bearish counterattack line. Notice how the second candle gapped open over the real body of the first on June 4, 2007, but reversed lower to close at exactly the same level as the white candle. A reversal lower was confirmed by the black candle on June 5 that gapped lower and never really recovered.

FIGURE 3-31

Counterattack Lines

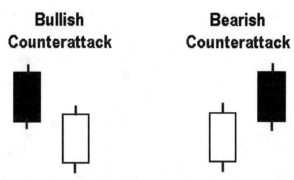

**Bullish
Counterattack**

**Bearish
Counterattack**

The counterattack or meeting lines are recognized by the second candle in the pattern. Black is bearish, white is bullish.

The counterattack lines provide momentary changes in trader psychology, but the failure to penetrate the real body makes these patterns slightly suspect. It is recommended that confirmation of the reversal occur in the direction of the second candle (i.e., a subsequent white candle in a bullish counterattack or a subsequent black candle in a bearish counterattack) before any trades are entered. Resistance is at the top of the bearish counterattack line, which means that a stop should be placed just above that level when one is trading this pattern. Support is at the low of the bullish counterattack line, which means that a stop should be placed just below that level when one is trading the pattern.

LONGER-TERM REVERSAL PATTERNS

These include the three mountain top, the related three Buddha top, the three river bottom, and the inverted three Buddha pattern.

Three Mountains and Three Rivers

These reversal patterns are longer term in nature, and the focus is not so much on the color or length of candles as it is on the level at

FIGURE 3-32

Bearish Counterattack Line for SPDR S&P Retail ETF, Daily

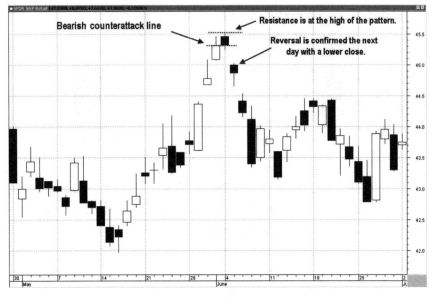

Source: MetaStock

which price reverses higher or lower. The principles of support and resistance are invoked with these patterns; this will be discussed in more detail in Chapter 5. The *three mountain top* is a more complex pattern that normally marks a longer-term top in the market. It is similar to the triple-top formation used in Western technical analysis. A three mountain top formation occurs when price fails to break through a resistance area on three separate occasions before reversing lower. Each of the three peaks can be in the same vicinity or heading lower as each successive peak weakens. A variation of the three mountain top is known as the *three Buddha top,* in which the center top of the three is the highest. This is the equivalent of the West's head and shoulders top. The three Buddha top gets its name from a Buddhist temple where one large Buddha is placed between two smaller Buddhas. Figure 3-33 shows three mountain and three Buddha tops.

The three mountain top pattern does not need all three highs to be at the same price level. Since these topping patterns take time

FIGURE 3-33

Three Mountain Top and Three Buddha Top Patterns

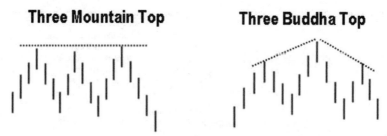

Three Mountain Top

Three Buddha Top

The three mountain top has three peaks at roughly the same level, whereas the three Buddha top has a higher center peak.

to develop, it is best to look for resistance in a range of prices as opposed to specific price levels. Figure 3-34, a daily chart of KLA-Tencor Corporation, shows how sellers emerged in the range of 68 to 70 three different times to push the price lower. Eventually their efforts caused price to reverse and begin a new downtrend. Also note the evening star pattern that formed on the third attempt to push through resistance. This showed that the third peak was a last-gasp effort by buyers to push the price higher before the reversal began in earnest.

Figure 3-35 shows a three Buddha top. The Dow Jones Industrial Average is shown in a weekly format from 2006 through 2008. This was the final market top before the 2008 market meltdown. Note how price pushed out to a new high in July 2007 at peak 1. After a sharp sell-off into August, price pushed out to a new high in October 2007, which formed a spinning top at peak 2, which warned of a potential price reversal. Large black candles formed in two of the next four weeks, showing that sellers were unloading shares. After one final weak push higher to peak 3, a final spinning top formed, showing that buyers lacked the resolve to push price back up to its previous high. The subsequent reversal began one of the worst periods in stock market history. It is interesting to note that the reversal off each peak began immediately after the

FIGURE 3-34

Three Mountain Top Pattern for Kla-Tencor Corporation, Daily

Source: MetaStock

formation of a spinning top, showing indecision as buyers tried to push prices higher.

A *three river bottom* is similar to the triple bottom in Western technical analysis, and the *inverted three Buddha* pattern is similar to the West's inverted head and shoulders pattern. Figure 3-36 shows an example of each.

Again, look for the bottoms on the three river bottom pattern to occur in roughly the same price *range* as opposed to a set consistent value. Figure 3-37 of the daily NYSE Composite Index shows a three river bottom as price forms three straight lows (or troughs) in the range of 6900 to 7000 in April–May 2005. The candles at low 1 and low 3 each had a long lower shadow, which signified strong buying support as price entered the range of 6900 to 7000. Notice how the reversal higher off low 3 was confirmed by the formation of three white soldiers.

The inverted three Buddha pattern has the middle low or trough as its lowest point. The chart for daily crude oil in

FIGURE 3-35

Three Buddha Top Pattern for Dow Jones Industrial Average, Weekly

Source: MetaStock

Figure 3-38 illustrates that point. The first low (1) was formed in November 2006 before correcting into the December 2006 peak, The next push lower (2) was even stronger than the first, pushing crude oil to a new low for the decline. Notice the tight, congested cluster of candles at the January 2007 low, which showed that buyers and sellers were struggling over the near-term direction of prices. After another corrective bounce into March 2007, the third low (3) was nowhere near the low at 2, which showed that sellers had lost downside momentum and that buyers were taking control of the crude oil market.

When one is trading off these long developing patterns, it is best to place protective stops either below the third low off a bottom or above the third high off a top. Always be mindful of the distance between the trade entry price and the stop price to determine whether the risk exposure is worth the trade.

FIGURE 3-36

Three River Bottom and Inverted Three Buddha Pattern

Three River Bottom   **Inverted Three Buddha**

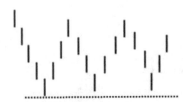 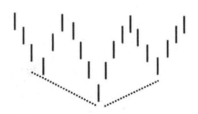

The three river bottom has three lows (or troughs) at roughly the same level, whereas the inverted three Buddha has a lower center trough.

FIGURE 3-37

Three River Bottom Pattern for NYSE Composite Index, Daily

Source: MetaStock

FIGURE 3-38

Inverted Three Buddha Pattern: Crude Oil, Daily

A tight, congested cluster of candles at the January 2007 low showed that a struggle was under way for price direction.

Source: MetaStock

TOWER TOPS AND BOTTOMS

Tower tops and bottoms occur after significant market moves. Their formation shows that a rather abrupt change in market psychology is unfolding. Tower reversal patterns resemble the V top or bottom in Western technical analysis. Figure 3-39 shows a tower top and a tower bottom.

Tower tops form after price has advanced and buyers seem to be in control. A long white candle appears, which is a bullish signal. After the white candle, a period of sideways price movement develops that shows indecision among traders as to the direction in which price should go. This behavior alone puts the continuation of the uptrend in doubt. After the brief period of indecision a long black candle forms, which shows that sellers are gaining control of the market. The daily chart of the Financial Select Sector SPDR ETF in Figure 3-40 shows a tower top. During this time, price was

FIGURE 3-39

Tower Top and Tower Bottom Patterns

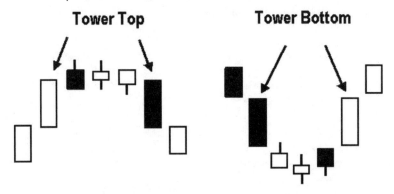

Tower Top   **Tower Bottom**

The combination of white and black candles in these patterns forms what looks like a tower.

FIGURE 3-40

Tower Top Pattern for Financial Select Sector SPDR ETF, Daily

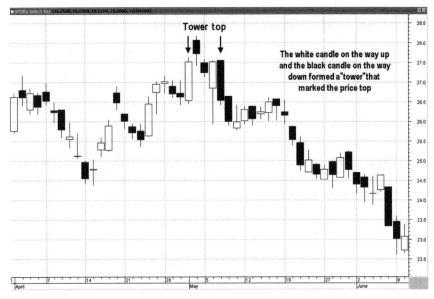

Source: MetaStock

chopping higher, making higher highs and higher lows after the March 2008 low. Price pushed higher with a long white candle forming on May 1, just one day before the May 2 high. A long black candle was formed on May 7 that formed the second half of the tower top. This showed that trader sentiment had changed as prices began to move lower.

Tower bottoms occur in a similar fashion to tower tops, only this time the first candle of the tower should be black, followed by a long white candle to signify a reversal higher. The period of indecision between the candles remains the same. Just as with tower tops, these types of reversals can be volatile and reflect rapidly shifting sentiment among traders. Crude oil is one market that tends to have its share of tower reversals. The daily chart of crude oil in Figure 3-41 shows an example of a tower bottom.

Note in Figure 3-41 how two of the four candles between the tower candles showed indecision among traders. The spinning top immediately after the long black candle showed a weakening of selling momentum. The doji two days later gave an even stronger

FIGURE 3-41

Tower Bottom Pattern for Crude Oil, Daily

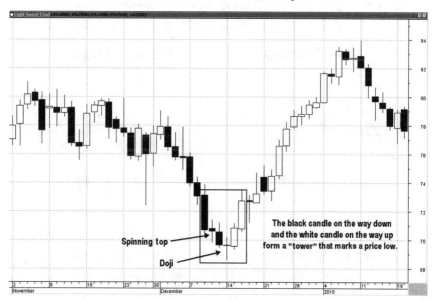

Source: MetaStock

indication that a bottom may have been reached. The tower bottom formation that was completed two days later provided confirmation that the doji formed on December 14, 2009, was indeed a major low.

DUMPLING TOPS AND FRY PAN BOTTOMS

A *dumpling top* is similar to a Western rounded top. It typically is composed of small real bodies that attempt to push higher but fail to do so, resulting in a rounded pattern that is confirmed with a gap lower as sellers take over. The color of the real bodies is not important in the formation. This formation is similar to the tower top except that it needs a gap lower to confirm the reversal. A fry pan bottom is similar to a Western rounded bottom. It also typically is composed of candles with small real bodies that create a rounded bottom appearance. A gap higher confirms a reversal out of this pattern. Figure 3-42 shows a dumpling top and a fry pan bottom.

FIGURE 3-42

Dumpling Top and Fry Pan Bottom Patterns

Dumpling Top   **Fry Pan Bottom**

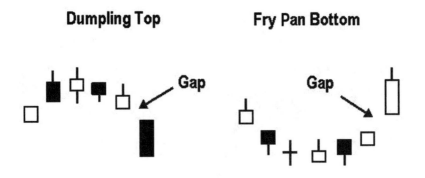

The color of the real bodies in the small candles forming the top or bottom is not important.

Dumpling tops give the appearance of a roller coaster reaching the top of a hill before accelerating lower. There just isn't a lot of upside momentum to continue pushing price higher, as indicated by the small real bodies on the candles forming the top. The gap lower is a signal that the top has been reached and downside acceleration is beginning. Since these tops take multiple candles to form, they usually have longer-term implications than the simpler reversal patterns discussed earlier in this chapter. The daily chart of Google in Figure 3-43 shows a dumpling top.

Fry pan bottoms display the same characteristics as dumpling tops, only at market lows. As price comes in to the low, selling interest wanes, as demonstrated by the small real bodies of the candles. A gap higher after the rounded bottom confirms the reversal. The daily chart of the U.S. Dollar Index in Figure 3-44 shows a fry pan bottom that formed in March 2003. Notice the small real bodies of the candles and the rounded bottom formation.

FIGURE 3-43

Dumpling Top Pattern for Google, Daily

Source: MetaStock

FIGURE 3-44

Fry Pan Bottom for U.S. Dollar Index, Daily

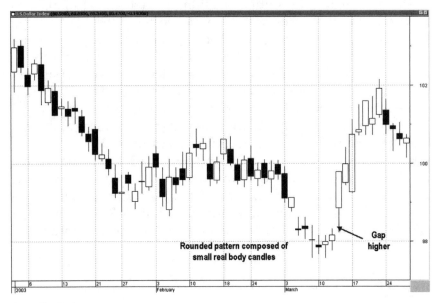

Source: MetaStock

SUMMARY

The patterns described in this chapter will serve you well as you use them to identify shifts in trader sentiment as buyers and sellers continually struggle for control of price direction. Traders are always attempting to buy low and sell high, but this is much easier said than done. Being able to take a step back and observe the daily battles as well as longer-term shifts in trader sentiment can make the difference between a winning and a losing trade. The key to interpreting and using these patterns is to remain flexible. For example, if you continually look for the perfect tower top, counterattack line, spinning top, and so on, you will miss out on some great trading opportunities. Of course the rules for each pattern need to be enforced, but the point is to not talk oneself out of a trade simply because a pattern is not perfect. Trading is a discipline that unfortunately entails some trial and error. If you can learn to identify key turning points in the market, however, this process should be less painful than trading is for those who wander blindly into the trading arena with little preparation.

CHAPTER 4

Candlestick Continuation Patterns

Chapter 3 examined reversal patterns and the trader mindset behind them. This chapter will discuss candle lines and combinations that demonstrate that a trend is likely to continue. A *continuation pattern* is one that shows the likelihood of a trend continuing in the same direction in which it was going before the continuation pattern was formed. In many cases continuation patterns allow for safer trade entry than do reversal patterns since continuation patterns reinforce a trend that already exists. Trading with the prevailing trend as often as possible allows a trader to hitch a free ride on the energy that already is driving the market. Since the development of a continuation pattern represents a period of rest for price movement, it is best to be patient *while* a continuation pattern is forming, waiting until the pattern resolves itself in the direction of the prevailing trend before initiating a new trading position.

As with reversal patterns, it is also wise to have the overall picture of the market. For example, is a continuation pattern forming just above support or just below resistance? Knowing where the pattern is developing in relation to important market levels can help determine whether a trade should be taken. As was noted at the end of Chapter 3, it is important to have some degree of flexibility to recognize the candlestick patterns with regard to their formation as opposed to looking for the perfect textbook candlestick example. Looking for a perfect candlestick pattern can cause a trader to miss good trading opportunities. Not every example shown in this chapter will be a perfect textbook example that results in the clean continuation of a strong trend. The point here is that the mere appearance of a continuation pattern by itself is not enough of a reason to initiate a new position. It is always best to wait for proof that the trend is resuming before entering a trade. Real life trading is always throwing curveballs, and the quicker you learn to adjust to what the market is telling you, the more effective a trader you will be.

WINDOWS

A *window* in candlestick charting is the same as a *gap* in Western technical analysis terminology. It is an open spot or break on a price chart that occurs between the closing price of one day and the opening price of the next. When a gap is formed, it is known in candlestick terminology as opening the window, and when the gap is filled, it is known as closing the window. An upside gap is known as a *rising window,* and a downside gap is known as a *falling window.*

    The window is viewed as a continuation pattern because the gap area becomes support (rising window) or resistance (falling window) as price retraces in an attempt to close the window. If the window area is breached in the opposite direction, price behavior is showing signs of a reversal. One of the great qualities of windows is that they specify a very unambiguous level at which a stop loss should be set. If the stop loss is triggered, the reason for taking the trade in the first place (an open window) no longer exists, which increases the odds that the trend could reverse. It is important to note that a window is formed when one candle opens completely out of the range of the prior candle. This means that shadows are included in the determination, not just real bodies. The color of the candles is not as important as the appearance of the window itself. Figure 4-1 shows rising and falling windows.

    Rising windows in an uptrend signify that the trend is healthy and buying pressure is strong. The daily chart of Google in Figure 4-2 shows multiple rising windows in a healthy uptrend. One of the rising windows was closed, which momentarily

F I G U R E   4 - 1

Rising and Falling Windows

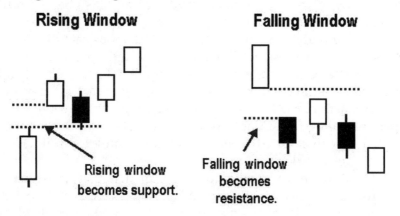

F I G U R E   4 - 2

Rising Windows for Google, Daily

Source: MetaStock

increased the odds for a trend reversal, but buyers quickly reentered the market. The two candles that followed the closing of the window were a spinning top and then a bullish belt hold that signaled the resumption of the uptrend.

Falling windows in a downtrend demonstrate the selling pressure that is present, showing the strength of the trend. The daily chart of Cisco Systems, Inc., in Figure 4-3 is a great example of multiple falling windows that show sellers in firm control of the price action. Notice how all but one of the windows remained open, revealing the strength of the trend. The bounce that closed the window in early 2011 ended with a spinning top followed by a long black candle.

Windows have great importance in that they are typically emotional events that are driven by traders' response to news stories, world political events, or earnings announcements of particular companies. The support and/or resistance areas created by

FIGURE 4-3

Falling Windows for Cisco Systems, Inc., Daily

Source: MetaStock

opening windows must be considered when one is analyzing other candlestick patterns for potential success or failure. When you are looking to enter a trade in the direction of the trend, place your stop just below the lower end of the window in an uptrend or just above the upper end of the window in a downtrend.

TASUKI

A *tasuki* is a rare two-candle pattern that forms after the opening of a window. An *upward tasuki gap* is composed of a white candle gapping higher (rising window) followed by a black candle. The black candle should open within the real body of the white candle and close below the white candle's real body. A *downward tasuki gap* is made by a downward-gapping black candle (falling window) followed by a white candle. The white candle should open within the real body of the black candle and close above the real body of the black candle. In either case, the two candles should be about the same size. This pattern uses the principle of an open window providing support or resistance. Figure 4-4 shows upward-gapping and downward-gapping tasuki gaps.

The daily chart of Cohen & Steers Realty Trust ETF in Figure 4-5 shows an upward tasuki gap. A rising window was formed by a white candle, followed by a black candle that was unable to

FIGURE 4-4

Tasuki Gaps

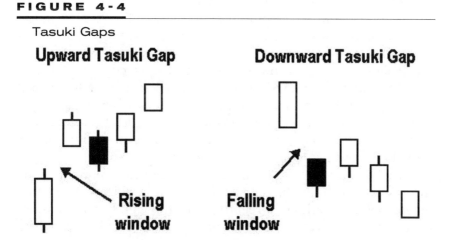

Upward Tasuki Gap

Downward Tasuki Gap

Rising window

Falling window

FIGURE 4-5

Upward Tasuki Gap Failure for Cohen & Steers Realty Trust
ETF, Daily

close the window. This window was closed rather quickly on the
next trading day, which resulted in a short, sharp correction, but
the uptrend eventually resumed. This is an example of what could
be considered a tasuki gap failure, but it also illustrates a strong
resumption of the trend as the November 27 falling window was
closed the next trading day by a long white candle on November 30. This was a very strong signal that the uptrend was resuming.

The daily chart of IBM in Figure 4-6 shows a downward
tasuki gap. In this instance, the gap was filled rather quickly by a
gravestone doji, which hardly inspired the bulls. This illustrates
the power of the doji pattern as the downtrend resumed in spite of
the falling window being closed on only the second day.

The appearance of a tasuki pattern is not as important as the
gap itself. A rising or falling window is an important event that
should not be overlooked regardless of the candle patterns that
surround it. Always remember that a falling window provides

FIGURE 4-6

Downward Tasuki Gap for IBM, Daily

The falling window was closed, but by a gravestone doji, meaning there was more downside to come.

Source: MetaStock

resistance whereas a rising window provides support. The focus should always be on whether the window remains open or is closed and, if it is closed, what type of candle closed the window. As was shown in Figure 4-6, a falling window closed by a bearish candle (gravestone doji) does not carry the same weight as it would if the window had been closed by a bullish long white candle. When one is looking to trade tasuki gaps, stop placement should be the same as with normal windows, using the extremes of the window as a guide.

GAPPING PLAYS

A *high price gapping play* is a pattern that forms after a sharp advance. Its name is derived from the fact that price forms a rising window at or very near a price high. After a long white candle, price consolidates near the high with a group of small real body candles. The fact that price is consolidating near the high instead of reversing lower is a bullish condition on its own, but when that consolidation is followed by a rising window, the result is a strong continuation pattern.

A *low price gapping play* is the opposite of a high price gapping play and is a pattern that forms after a sharp decline. Its name is derived from the fact that price forms a falling window at or very near a price low. After a long black candle, price consolidates near the low with a group of small real body candles. The formation of a falling window after the consolidation shows that price is ready to continue lower. Figure 4-7 shows gapping plays.

High price gapping plays show strong upside momentum as a white candle is formed and the gains are held as price consolidates sideways within the white candle. This pattern shows a bullish bias among traders as there is insufficient selling pressure to push price significantly lower off its high. The rising window that follows is a strong signal that the uptrend is ready to resume. The daily chart of Amazon.com in Figure 4-8 shows an example

FIGURE 4-7

Gapping Plays

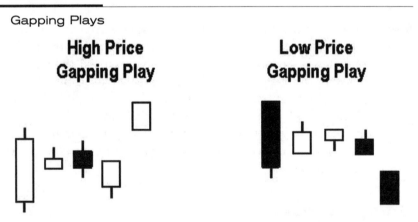

**High Price
Gapping Play**

**Low Price
Gapping Play**

**The color and type of candles in the consolidation
phase are not important. Watch for the gap higher
or lower to signal continuation.**

FIGURE 4-8

High Price Gapping Play for Amazon.com, Daily

Source: MetaStock

of a high price gapping play. Notice how price exploded sharply higher out of this pattern.

A low price gapping play shows a continuation of a down-trend as bearish sentiment forces price lower. After a sharp decline in the form of a black candle, price consolidates as there is very little buying pressure to reverse the trend. The appearance of the falling window after consolidation shows that the downtrend is resuming as sellers continue to unload shares. The daily chart of the Financial Select Sector SPDR ETF in Figure 4-9 shows a low price gapping play. Note how the falling window acted as resistance as price bounced after the falling window was formed. When one is trading high or low price gapping plays, a stop can be placed in the same way as in the previous examples at the extreme of the gaps. If the gap is filled, continuation of the trend becomes suspect.

FIGURE 4-9

Low Price Gapping Play For Financial Select Sector SPDR
ETF, Daily

Source: MetaStock

RISING OR FALLING THREE METHODS

The rising and falling three methods are also continuation patterns
that contain sharp price moves followed by a period of price consolidation. These patterns represent a resting phase after a sharp
price move and are similar to Western patterns such as the flag and
the Gann pullback. Just as with a gapping play, there is a "quiet"
period that is followed by a resumption of the prevailing trend.
Figure 4-10 shows the rising and falling three methods.

The *rising three method* consists of a long white candle followed
by a period of price consolidation within the real body of the white
candle. The three candles should be black and should form a
downward pattern. There is some flexibility with the pattern as in
powerful uptrends there may be only two candles during consolidation before price explodes higher, whereas at other times there
can be more than three candles if the consolidation period takes a

FIGURE 4-10

Rising and Falling Three Methods

Rising Three Method   Falling Three Method

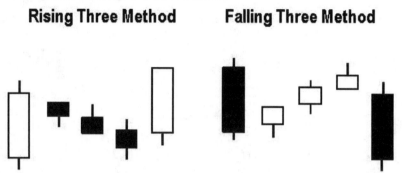

This method can consist of at least two or more than three "consolidation" candles and still be valid.

bit longer. Also, it is *preferred* that the consolidation candles form a downward pattern, but as long as they are contained within the real body of the white candle, the pattern can be considered valid. The key to the pattern is a strong resumption of the uptrend with another white candle after the consolidation phase. The daily chart of Zimmer Holdings in Figure 4-11 shows an example of the rising three method. Notice the small real bodies during the consolidation and also note that the third candle during consolidation (circled) was a spinning top, showing indecision, which gave more weight to the following white candle as the brief period of indecision had been resolved.

The *falling three method* consists of a long black candle followed by a period of price consolidation within the real body of the black candle. It is preferred that the three candles be white and form an upward pattern. As with the rising three method, there is some flexibility in that the consolidation phase can consist of two or more candles. The key to this pattern is also a strong resumption of the trend with another black candle after the consolidation phase. The daily chart of the Nasdaq Composite Index in Figure 4-12

FIGURE 4-11

Rising Three Method for Zimmer Holdings, Daily

Source: MetaStock

shows the falling three method. Note the small real bodies during the consolidation.

The rising and falling three methods are reliable continuation patterns as they show a market that makes a sharp move and then takes a breather before continuing in the direction of the original move. The key to identifying this pattern is recognizing multiple harami that form within the real body of the first candle. A resumption of price movement in the direction of the first long candle of the pattern signifies a strong trend. Trade entry on a rising or falling three method can introduce a higher degree of risk in stop placement since the pattern begins at the extreme price of the first candle of the pattern. With a rising three method, the stop should be placed below the first long white candle of the pattern. With a falling three method, the stop should be placed above the top of the first long black candle of the pattern.

FIGURE 4-12

Falling Three Method for the Nasdaq Composite Index, Daily

Another push lower
followed this pattern.

Source: MetaStock

SEPARATING LINES

Separating lines are strong continuation patterns that use a principle similar to that of the counterattack line pattern that was covered in Chapter 3. The difference is that instead of looking for the same or a similar *closing* price as with counterattack lines, one should look for the same or a similar *opening* price between the two opposite-colored candles. This shows resolve on the part of buyers (bullish separating lines) or sellers (bearish separating lines) as price gaps to the open of the previous candle. Figure 4-13 shows separating lines.

Bullish separating lines show a resolve among buyers as demand forms a rising gap from the closing price of the previous black candle to the opening price of that candle. This indicates strong demand for a security at current price levels. Whether that demand is due to a breaking news story, an earnings report, or simple valuation is not as important as the reaction shown by traders as

FIGURE 4-13
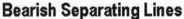

Separating Lines

Bullish Separating Lines   Bearish Separating Lines

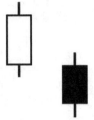

It is important for the opening prices to be the same or very close. Do not bypass this pattern just because the opening prices are not an exact match.

enough demand is generated to gap the price higher. The signal is stronger if the first black candle is a long candle, which shows even more resolve among buyers as price has to move that much farther to reach the previous candle's opening price. It is also a very strong signal if the second candle has an opening marubozu (or shaven bottom), which means that the action opened at the low and never looked back. The daily chart of the Financial Select Sector SPDR ETF in Figure 4-14 shows bullish separating lines. Notice how the second circled example shows an example of using a black candle with a small real body. That makes the next day's opening price less impressive because of a smaller gap higher, but it is also in the middle of a very strong push higher. Again, each pattern must be examined within the context in which it appears on the chart. In this case there was a lot of upside energy already showing itself in the uptrend, which gave the pattern more validity.

Bearish separating lines show a continuation of downtrends as price gaps lower to the opening price of the previous white candle. This shows strong resolve among sellers, which drives the price lower. Just as in bullish separating lines, this pattern carries

FIGURE 4-14

Bullish Separating Lines For Financial Select Sector SPDR
ETF, Daily

Source: MetaStock

more weight if there is an opening marubozu as price opens at its
high for the session and moves lower from there. The daily chart
of Citigroup in Figure 4-15 shows bearish separating lines. This
chart shows a small white candle as the first half of the pattern,
which makes the second candle's open less impressive, but notice
the conditions under which the bearish separating lines appear.
Price had been correcting in a weak push higher, as shown by the
contracting body sizes of the candles. Since very little energy was
being expended among buyers on the upward push, the path of
least resistance was still lower.

Although separating lines are primarily continuation patterns,
their appearance after a strong advance (bearish separating lines)
or decline (bullish separating lines) also can be an indication of a
price reversal. The key is to recognize the pattern and be flexible
enough to use it even though consecutive opening prices may not
be an exact match.

FIGURE 4-15

Bearish Separating Lines for Citigroup, Daily

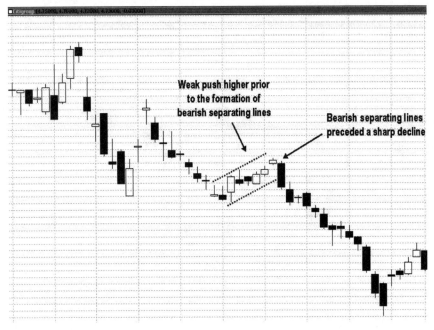

Source: MetaStock

NECK LINES

Neck lines are patterns that are weaker variations of a bullish piercing line or dark cloud cover. Whereas those patterns are strong reversal signals, neck lines are continuation patterns in that the second candle could not muster enough strength to generate a valid reversal signal. Think of neck lines as failed reversal attempts.

Bullish in neck lines begin the same way as a dark cloud cover. Price must be in an uptrend and then gap higher over the previous white candle before trading lower to close at the same closing price as the previous candle. Its appearance gives sellers pause as the push lower was not able to penetrate the real body of the previous white candle.

Bearish in neck lines begin the same way as a bullish piercing line. Price must be in a downtrend and then gap lower beneath the

FIGURE 4-16

In Neck Lines

Bullish in Neck Line   **Bearish in Neck Line**

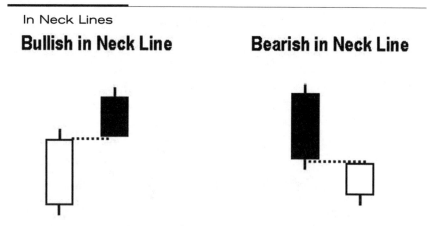

The in neck line closes at or very close to the previous candle's close.

previous black candle before trading higher to close at the same closing price as the previous black candle. This formation causes buyers to rethink their positions as buying pressure for the session was not able to penetrate the body of the previous black candle. Figure 4-16 shows in neck lines.

The daily chart of the Technology Select Sector SPDR ETF in Figure 4-17 shows a bullish in neck line. Remember, this is a continuation pattern since it is a weak version of the dark cloud cover as a result of its inability to penetrate the real body of the previous white candle. Notice how price gapped up over the previous white candle but failed to close within its real body.

Bearish in neck lines show continuation in a downtrend, as shown in the daily chart of the Consumer Discretionary Select Sector SPDR ETF in Figure 4-18. Price gapped lower but failed to close within the real body of the previous black candle, which was a signal that the conviction among buyers was probably not strong enough to trigger a meaningful price reversal. Sure enough, the downtrend continued.

Bullish on neck lines develop the same way as bullish in neck lines; the only difference is the close. In this case the close is at or

FIGURE 4-17

Bullish in Neck Lines for Technology Select Sector SPDR
ETF, Daily

Source: MetaStock

near the low of the day. This means that if the second candle has
a lower shadow, the second candle price *close* must be at or near
the upper end of the first candle's shadow. If there is a closing
marubozu on the previous white candle (no upper shadow), this
pattern is very similar to a bullish in neck line since the closing
price represents the upper boundary of the white candle's real
body. Figure 4-19 shows on neck lines.

Bullish on neck lines represent a lack of the real selling
pressure that would be needed to signal a reversal. Since the gains
from the previous white candle have been held relative to the
closing price, there is little reason for recent buyers to get nervous
and rethink their positions. The daily chart of the Energy Select
Sector SPDR ETF in Figure 4-20 shows how a bullish on neck line
looks and how it can signal a continuation of the trend. After the
on neck line, price consolidated for two days before the uptrend
resumed.

F I G U R E   4 - 1 8

Bearish in Neck Lines for Consumer Discretionary Select
Sector SPDR ETF, Daily

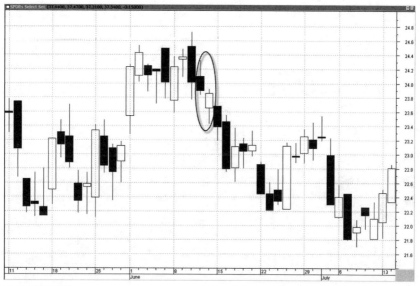

Source: MetaStock

F I G U R E   4 - 1 9

On Neck Lines

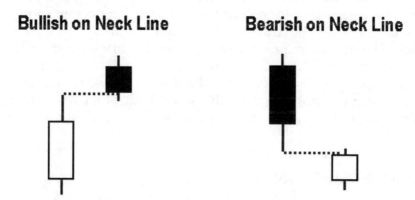

Bullish on Neck Line   **Bearish on Neck Line**

**On neck lines close at or near the high or low of
the previous candle.**

FIGURE 4-20

Bullish on Neck Line for Energy Select Sector SPDR ETF,
Daily

Source: MetaStock

The bearish on neck line forms in a downtrend and also
signals downtrend continuation as buyers—even though they held
the line with regard to the gap lower open—were not able to get
the price to close above the previous day's low price. This shows a
lack of buying pressure, which is an indication that the trend is not
ready to reverse. The daily chart of D.R. Horton, Inc., in Figure 4-21
illustrates a bearish on neck line. The close of the second candle in
the pattern was not able to touch the real body of the first candle,
which signaled buying weakness just before a resumption of the
downtrend.

THRUSTING LINES

Thrusting lines also are seen as undeveloped bullish piercing lines
or dark cloud covers, but they differ from neck lines because they
do penetrate the real body of the previous candle, though not past

FIGURE 4-21

Bearish on Neck Line for D.R. Horton, Inc., Daily

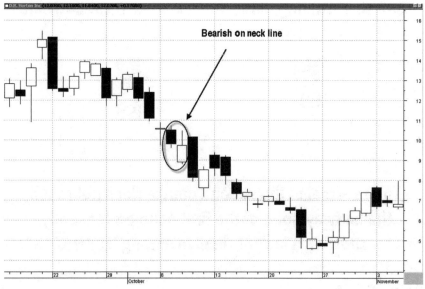

Source: MetaStock

the halfway point necessary to signal a reversal. Although these lines have slightly stronger reversal characteristics than do neck lines, their failure to penetrate over half of the prior candle's real body shows that a continuation of the trend is likely. Figure 4-22 shows thrusting lines.

When a bullish thrusting pattern begins to develop in an uptrend, it closely resembles the dark cloud cover pattern in that it gaps higher over the high of the previous white candle and then reverses lower. The difference is that sellers lack enough conviction to give buyers pause, which fails to deter buying pressure. As buyers recognize that sellers are not participating aggressively, there is less fear of loss, and that brings more buyers into the market. The daily chart of Google in Figure 4-23 shows a bullish thrusting line. What started out as an ominous sign with a potential dark cloud cover turned out to be inspirational to buyers because selling pressure was not strong enough to cause a meaningful penetration of the previous white candle's real body.

FIGURE 4-22

Thrusting Lines

Bullish Thrusting Line   ## Bearish Thrusting Line

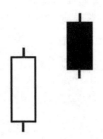 

The reversal of the second candle does not reach the halfway point of the first candle's real body, showing a lack of resolve among traders

FIGURE 4-23

Bullish Thrusting Line for Google, Daily

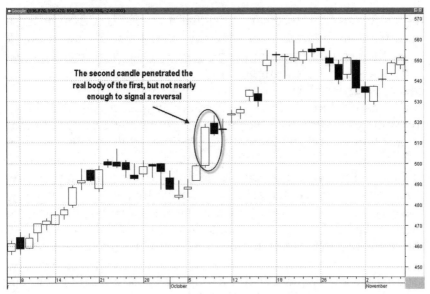

Source: MetaStock

FIGURE 4-24

Bearish Thrusting Line for Technology Select Sector SPDR ETF, Daily

Source: MetaStock

The daily chart of Technology Select Sector SPDR ETF in Figure 4-24 shows a bearish thrusting line. The downtrend in force and the formation of the bearish thrusting line showed that buyers were not showing enough conviction to turn the tide or force price higher.

Although neck lines and thrusting lines are classified as continuation patterns, I have looked at enough charts and situations to know that these lines need confirmation of trend resumption (a long white candle in an uptrend or a long black candle in a downtrend) to confirm that the trend indeed is continuing. Also be aware of where these lines form. If a bullish neck or thrusting line forms at a resistance area, the odds of a failure of the continuation pattern increase. If a bearish neck or thrusting line appears at support, the odds of a failure increase there as well.

SIDE BY SIDE LINES

Side by side lines are three-candle patterns that can be either bullish or bearish, depending on the context in which they appear. Each pattern starts with a gap or window being opened, followed by side by side candles of the same color. The significance of this pattern is that it shows profit taking after a strong move as price action pauses before resuming in the direction of the gap and the trend.

Bullish side by side white lines form in an uptrend with an initial white candle followed by a rising window. After the window is opened, two white candles are formed that are side by side, signifying that the window will remain open, which is bullish for the trend. The two white candles should be similar in opening prices and real body size. The second white candle shows that sellers initially tried to close the window demonstrated by the gap lower open to match the previous white candle. Buyers come into the market again, however, providing evidence that there is enough demand to keep the window open.

Bearish side by side white lines occur in a downtrend that follows a black candle and a falling window. Once the window is opened, two white candles form side by side. The difference here is that the two candles open below the falling window and reverse higher but not enough to close the window. This shows that there is not enough buying conviction to close the window, which is an indication that the downtrend probably will resume. Remember, a rising window provides support and a falling window provides resistance. The longer the windows remain open, the stronger their support or resistance becomes. Figure 4-25 shows side by side white lines.

The daily chart of iShares Barclay's 20+ Year Treasury Bond Fund ETF in Figure 4-26 shows bullish side by side white lines. This chart shows the resolve of buyers, which signals a strong uptrend. After the side by side lines, price consolidated with an upward bias, which showed an unwillingness among sellers to part with their shares. This showed strong bullishness among traders. Price rose from $112 to $122 in two weeks.

Bearish side by side white lines in a downtrend show the resolve of sellers as the falling window is not closed despite being

FIGURE 4-25

Side by Side White Lines

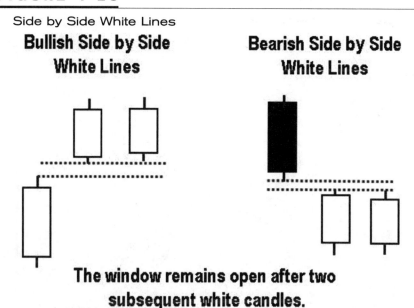

Bullish Side by Side White Lines

Bearish Side by Side White Lines

The window remains open after two subsequent white candles.

FIGURE 4-26

Side by Side White Lines for Ishares Barclay's 20+ Year Treasury Bond Fund ETF, Daily

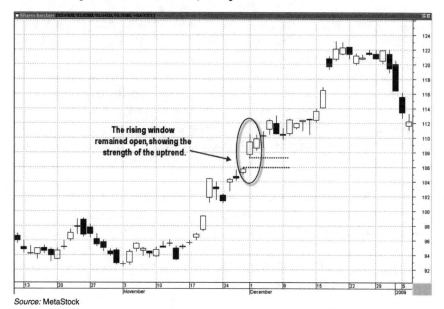

The rising window remained open, showing the strength of the uptrend.

Source: MetaStock

FIGURE 4-27

Bearish Side by Side White Lines for Google, Daily

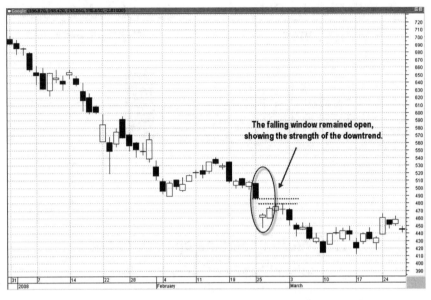

followed by two white candles. A very strong downtrend was in place in the daily chart of Google shown in Figure 4-27. Price gapped lower in late February, followed by two white candles that were unable to close the window. The next two candles were very interesting: The buyers won the day for a third straight day but still were not able to close the falling window. The fourth day formed a doji, which signaled that the upside correction probably had ended. Four straight small body candles were unable to close the window, which signaled that the downtrend was ready to continue.

Side by side black lines have the same bullish or bearish characteristics as side by side white lines. The importance of the pattern lies in the fact that a window remains open two trading days after being opened. It also demonstrates that traders probably are banking profits after a sharp price move as price rests before continuing the prevailing trend.

Bullish side by side black lines occur when a rising window is opened after a white candle in an uptrend. After the opening of the rising window, two subsequent black candles are formed that are similar in real body size and closing price. The fact that sellers could not close the rising window for two straight sessions is bullish and shows a lack of conviction among sellers.

Bearish side by side black lines occur when a falling window is opened after a black candle in a downtrend. After the opening of the falling window, two subsequent black candles are formed that open at or near the high for the session and trade lower into the close. The two candles are similar in real body size and closing price. The fact that sellers intervened to prevent the falling window from closing is bearish and shows that buyers lack enough conviction to cause a price reversal. Figure 4-28 shows side by side black lines.

An example of bullish side by side black lines is shown in the daily chart of SNDK–SanDisk Corporation in Figure 4-29. Notice how the rising window was not closed after two trading days.

FIGURE 4-28

Side by Side Black Lines

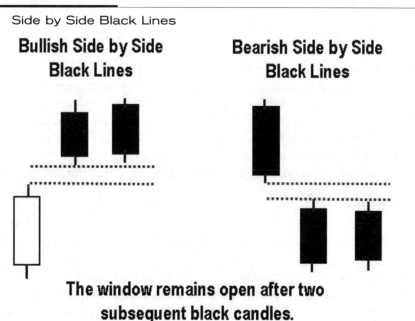

Bullish Side by Side Black Lines

Bearish Side by Side Black Lines

The window remains open after two subsequent black candles.

FIGURE 4-29

Bullish Side by Side Black Lines for SanDisk Corporation,
Daily

Source: MetaStock

Price consolidated in the same area, which provided evidence that
the two days of selling was likely due to profit taking and not due
to nervous longs dumping their shares. This example also shows
how a continuation pattern heading into a resistance area does not
provide much upside. As price neared the previous high around
46 that was posted in January 2007, one hanging man and two long
upper shadows formed. Price was stuck in a trading range just
below the previous high before it broke down three weeks later,
eventually resulting in a reversal as the rising window was closed.

Bearish side by side black lines show that there is insufficient
buying pressure to close a falling window as prices open at or
near their high for the day before moving lower as sellers resume
control. The second candle after the falling window shows that
sellers are locking in profits as price gaps higher near the opening
of the previous day. After that open, sellers resume control, driving

price lower to match the previous candle's close. This discourages any potential buyers, and the downtrend continues.

The daily chart of the Consumer Discretionary Select Sector SPDR ETF in Figure 4-30 shows bearish side by side black lines. The two black candles that formed after the falling window were quite long and showed heightened trading activity. The fact that the falling window remained open after two active trading days was bearish as price continued to fall for three more trading days. A bottom was formed a short time later, but the bearish side by side black lines alerted any traders looking for a bottom to be cautious and wait for signs of a reversal such as the hammer that formed on March 14. The hammer formed at the same level as the inverted hammer a week and a half earlier (on March 5) that showed good support.

FIGURE 4-30

Bearish Side by Side Black Lines for Consumer Discretionary Select Sector SPDR ETF, Daily

Source: MetaStock

SUMMARY

Each of the continuation patterns presented in this chapter can provide insight into the mindset and emotion of traders. It is always important, however, to examine each pattern within the context of where it appears. I cannot stress enough how important this is. Is a continuation pattern developing near resistance in an uptrend or near support in a downtrend? If that is the case, it must be viewed as suspect and traded with caution, if at all. The basic reversal and continuation patterns covered in the last two chapters form the foundation of sound candlestick chart analysis. Now it is time to move on to show the synergy of cultures by combining Japanese candlestick charting with Western technical analysis.

PART 2

From Japan to Wall Street: Using Candlestick Patterns with Western Techniques

Technical Analysis: Trends, Support, and Resistance

In the last three chapters the foundation was laid to construct, understand, and interpret candlestick lines and the patterns they form. Although those chapters made for some rather dry reading, they need to be studied and understood to establish a foundation for the development of solid trading techniques that can lead to profits and keep traders out of trouble. This chapter will show how the ancient methodology of candlestick charting can be combined with the more recent techniques developed in Western technical analysis.

Chapter 1 supplied a brief overview of technical analysis. It is important at this juncture to reestablish what technical analysis is *not*. Technical analysis is not some form of divine prophecy or a crystal ball. I cringe when I see some of the things posted on the Internet by "technicians." Plotting a price chart with a stochastic oscillator at the bottom does not allow someone to make informed market calls. Predictions should be viewed with a skeptical eye. No one has the ability to tell you exactly where prices will be tomorrow, one week from now, one month from now, or one year from now. Technical analysis is a discipline that requires constant attention because market dynamics are always changing, regularly morphing into new scenarios. A good technician understands this and is willing to look at new ideas or techniques and decide whether those techniques fit his or her individual trading style.

As was stated in Chapter 2, markets are living, breathing entities that feed on the losses of traders. Trading is a daily battle for which one must prepare. It is in this daily preparation that profits are made or lost. The goal of Chapters 5 through 7 is to introduce you to common standard technical analysis techniques and demonstrate that when technical analysis is paired with candlestick charting, a synergy far greater than the sum of the parts can be achieved. This synergy will serve us well because we are all traders whether we admit it or not. If a position is taken in the market, a profit or loss cannot be realized until that position is closed out. It doesn't matter if that position was held for a few minutes or a few weeks; the same two transactions had to occur to initiate and then close out the trade. It is when you enter and exit that makes the difference between winning and losing no matter what time frame you trade.

Technical analysis is about probabilities and tilting the odds in your favor by using reasonable market analysis. Nothing is 100 percent guaranteed, and so it is important always to have an exit plan in place in case your analysis is incorrect. The markets are made up of the collective will of traders, and this introduces an element of human emotion. Even in this era of automated trading, the human element lends a degree of unpredictability to even the most astute analysis. It is always important to be aware of shifts in trader emotion or sentiment that can make the difference between a profit and a loss. The purpose of this chapter is to examine the basics of technical analysis so that you will have a foundation for the development of your own methodologies.

SUPPORT AND RESISTANCE

Support and *resistance* are terms that refer to lines or zones on a chart that prevent price from falling lower (support) or rising higher (resistance). The psychology behind these price levels is deeper than that, however.

Price falls as a result of an oversupply of shares or futures contracts for sale that is not readily absorbed by willing buyers (demand). Price will continue to fall until buyers step up to increase demand to meet the excess supply. Support is a price level or range at which traders see good value in a security and enter the market to buy shares (equities) or contracts (futures); this prevents price from falling further. Support levels are formed in horizontal zones or as upsloping lines (either trendlines or price moving averages) that occur during uptrends. Horizontal support areas generally show accumulation of shares or contracts by buyers at a level of perceived value, whereas upsloping support areas (trendlines) show increased demand for a security that pushes the price higher. For now we will concentrate on flat or horizontal support zones. Support areas in trends will be discussed in subsequent sections.

An area of support on a price chart is a place where downward movement in price stopped and reversed higher in the past. At prior support areas it is reasonable to *expect* price to reverse and move higher. It is reasonable to assume that demand will reemerge at the same level, but it is always safer to make sure that buyers do emerge to support the price before entering any trades. Support areas do not always hold, and when they are broken, it is an indication that trader sentiment has taken a negative turn.

In the daily chart of the Energy Select Sector SPDR ETF in Figure 5-1, notice how price found support four times near the

FIGURE 5-1

Support Area for Energy Select Sector SPDR ETF, Daily

Source: MetaStock

24 level (the shaded area on the chart). That was an indication that buyers saw good value at that price and that shares were being accumulated. In each of the first three trips down into the support zone, the candles had long tails, which signaled that selling force (supply) was being met with greater buying force (demand). Simply put, demand was stronger than supply near the 24 level. Now take a look at the fourth trip down into the support zone. In that instance, a spinning top was formed that did not penetrate the support zone as deeply as the previous three instances had. That was a sure indication that selling pressure was weakening (less supply) and that buyers were in a position to begin a new push higher in price as demand outstripped supply.

In Figure 5-1 the support area held, but if it had broken down, that would have been an indication that there was more supply on the market than demand to absorb it, resulting in lower prices. A very important concept to understand in this case is that once support is broken, it becomes resistant to any subsequent price advances. It is best described as follows: *What was once support is now resistance.*

The daily chart of the SPDR S&P Retail ETF in Figure 5-2 shows a breakdown through a prior support level (the shaded area) near the $37 level. Note the long black candle on the day price broke down through support, which demonstrated very strong selling pressure. After the break lower, the old support level became resistance. This resistance area is formed by those who might have purchased shares at the $37 level previously (when it was support), who are now happy to get out at or near breakeven. The extra shares coming onto the market from these sellers increase supply enough to act as a barrier to price advances.

Resistance is a price level or range in which sellers appear that keeps price from advancing further. Just as with support areas, resistance areas can come in flat areas or in downsloping lines such as trendlines or moving averages. Since trendlines and moving averages are complex topics, they will be discussed later in this chapter.

Prior resistance areas are price levels that the price has been unable to penetrate, causing it to move lower. These levels can be *expected* to provide overhead resistance when encountered. As with support levels, it is important to make sure that the resistance

FIGURE 5-2

Failed Support Area for SPDR S&P Retail ETF, Daily

Source: MetaStock

level holds before selling your own shares or initiating a short position. Resistance levels are created by traders selling shares that cannot be absorbed readily by willing buyers. This situation causes a supply imbalance, which means that price has to move lower until sufficient demand is shown from buyers to stop price from declining.

The daily chart of the U.S. Dollar Index in Figure 5-3 shows how an overhead resistance area prevented price from moving any higher. In the shaded resistance area, notice that as price moved into it for the second time, reversal candles were formed. A shooting star followed by a long black candle, which formed a bearish engulfing pattern right in the resistance zone, showed that sellers were active, making it highly unlikely that price would break up through resistance. This ultimately led to a sharp price decline.

FIGURE 5-3

Resistance Area for U.S. Dollar Index, Daily

Source: MetaStock

What if a resistance area fails and price breaks up through that level? If you guessed that the former resistance now becomes support, you are correct. The dynamic is just the opposite of what it is with failed support. Those traders who shorted the market at or near the resistance zone are sitting on losses on the breakout. As price retreats to prior resistance from above, late shorts cover (or buy back) their positions, resulting in upward pressure on price. The breakout point also is viewed by traders as a lower-risk place from which to initiate long positions.

The daily chart of the U.S. Dollar Index in Figure 5-4 shows a breakout through resistance in December 2009. Note the long white candle on the breakout, demonstrating the conviction of buyers as price moved higher. Further proof that the new support area was likely to hold came in the form of a small bodied spinning top as price retreated back to the breakout level. The next day a long white candle formed, providing confirmation that the new support level would hold.

FIGURE 5-4

Failed Resistance Area That Is Now Support: U.S. Dollar
Index, Daily

Source: MetaStock

RETRACEMENT LEVELS

A *retracement* is a price movement in the opposite direction of the
previous trend. Retracements also are referred to as *pullbacks* as
traders of the previous trend exit the market to lock in profits. A
retracement level is a level at which price is expected to find support
(retracement from a price high) or resistance (retracement from
a price low). To compute retracement levels, a high price and a
low price for the previous trend are needed. There are different
methods for computing retracement levels. One of the most popular
methods among traders today is the use of Fibonacci ratios.

Fibonacci Levels

Fibonacci numbers are an integer series developed by the Italian
mathematician Leonard of Pisa around the year AD 1200. The
series starts with the number 1 and proceeds as follows: 1, 2, 3,

5, 8, 13, 21, 34, 55, 89, 144, 233, and so on. This series is simply a progression in which each number is the sum of the prior two numbers: $1 + 1 = 2$; $2 + 1 = 3$; $3 + 2 = 5$; $5 + 3 = 8$; $8 + 5 = 13$, and so on. It is also important to note that beginning with the number 34 in the sequence, each number is .618 of the *next* number: $34 = 55 \times .618$, $55 = 89 \times .618$, $89 = 144 \times .618$, and so forth. Also beginning with the number 34, the *next* number in the sequence is 1.618 of the preceding number: $34 = 21 \times 1.618$; $55 = 34 \times 1.618$; $89 = 55 \times 1.618$, and so on. Before the number 34, the ratios are very close to .618 or 1.618, but a degree of rounding is needed to achieve the constant relationship. The two numbers 0.618 and 1.618 are reciprocals to each other and can be used to compute other Fibonacci ratios. I could devote much more time to this fascinating topic, but that would be far beyond the scope of this book.

There are two types of Fibonacci price retracements: internal and external. For the purpose of our discussion we will concentrate on *internal* Fibonacci retracement levels of .382 (38.2 percent), .618 (61.8 percent), and .786 (78.6 percent). The halfway retracement level also will be used (.5, or 50 percent) even though it is not a Fibonacci number. It is an important level nonetheless as many times price finds support at a 50 percent retracement of its prior move. Although many software packages display Fibonacci retracement levels with a few mouse clicks, it is wise to take a few moments to explain how these levels are computed.

Let's say that Stock A rallies from $10 to $20 and begins a pullback. Since retracement levels are computed by using the range of the previous move, the first operation to perform is to subtract the low of the range from the high of the range ($20 - 10 = 10$). Next, compute the numerical values for each of the retracement levels by multiplying the range of the prior rally (in this case 10) by the percentage retracement desired. For a 38.2 percent retracement, multiply the range (10) by 38.2 percent, or .382. This yields a result of 3.82. For a 50 percent retracement, multiply the range (10) by 50 percent, or .5, which yields a value of 5. For a 61.8 percent retracement, multiply the range (10) by 61.8 percent, or .618, which yields 6.18. Finally, for a 78.6 percent retracement, multiply the range (10) by 78.6 percent, or .786, which yields a result of 7.86.

Now that the meaningful retracement values have been computed, subtract each one from the high point of the range (in this case 20), which gives specific price values to watch for support. The actual price levels are computed as shown in Table 5-1.

Using Table 5-1, once price begins to decline from $20, traders should watch for support at $16.18, $15.00, $13.82, and $12.14. Combining candlesticks with these retracement levels can give a trader an idea of whether price is likely to reverse direction at one of these retracement levels and resume the uptrend.

An example of a Fibonacci level at work is shown in the daily chart of the Energy Select Sector SPDR ETF in Figure 5-5. In the chart, only the 61.8 percent retracement level is shown so that the candlestick pattern and subsequent reversal in price are easier to see. First, note the lower and upper ends of the range as shown on the chart (arrows) as well as the computed 61.8 percent Fibonacci retracement level (44.05). Price retreated to the 61.8 percent retracement level, where potential reversal candles began to form. Notice how a spinning top was formed as price touched the 61.8 percent retracement level, immediately followed the next day by a doji. These were very important signs that selling pressure was weakening. Four days after the doji, a rising window was formed, signaling that trader conviction was such that the uptrend was ready to resume.

Fibonacci retracements in a downtrend are computed the same way except that the computed retracement values are *added* to the low value of the range. If the retracement levels for the stock described in Table 5-1 were computed after a *decline* from 20 to 10, the high/low range would remain the same ($20 - 10 = 10$), but the retracement levels would be computed as shown in Table 5-2.

Since Fibonacci retracements in a downtrend act as resistance, it is reasonable to believe that if a reversal candle line or candle

T a b l e   5 - 1

Price Level Computation

% Return	Computation	Price Level
38.2	20 – 3.82	16.18
50	20 – 5	15.00
61.8	20 – 6.18	13.82
78.6	20 – 7.86	12.14

Table 5-2

Retracement Levels

% Return	Computation	Price Level
38.2	20 + 3.82	13.82
50	20 + 5	15.00
61.8	20 + 6.18	16.18
78.6	20 + 7.86	17.86

pattern appears as price approaches one of these levels, a resumption of the downtrend can be expected. Remember however, that it is always prudent to wait for some form of confirmation of trend resumption before entering a trade on a Fibonacci retracement, such as the rising window in Figure 5-5.

FIGURE 5-5

Fibonacci Retracement in an Uptrend in Energy Select Sector SPDR ETF, Daily

Source: MetaStock

FIGURE 5-6

Fibonacci Retracement in a Downtrend for Cisco Systems, Daily

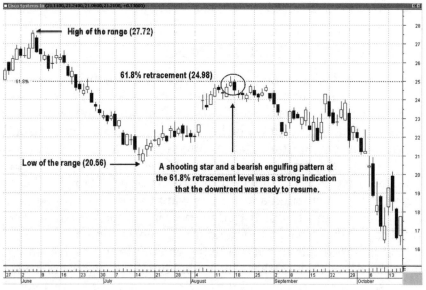

Source: MetaStock

The daily chart of Cisco Systems in Figure 5-6 shows a Fibonacci retracement level acting as resistance. Notice how price declined from June 5 to July 16, 2008, from a high of 27.72 to a low of 20.56. Again, since price reversed lower from the 61.8 percent retracement level, the other retracement level lines have been removed for readability. Notice how as price approached the 61.8 percent retracement level at 24.98, a shooting star formed, followed immediately by a bearish engulfing pattern. Price then chopped sideways for two weeks, forming a weak support area at the 24 level. On September 2, a black candle closed below the 24 level, signifying that price once again was beginning to break down. If a short trade had been entered on that breakdown, a trading stop could have been placed just above the 61.8 percent retracement level.

Although the mathematical theory behind the Fibonacci series is sound, be careful not to assume that support or resistance at these levels always will work. There is nothing magical about these levels as trader emotion can temporarily trump even the soundest concepts and principles. Always look for some form of confirmation by candlestick lines or patterns before making a reasonable assumption that a retracement level will hold.

CANDLESTICKS IN TRENDS

An additional filter that can help determine whether support or resistance is likely to hold is to measure the market trend. A market *trend* is best defined as the tendency of a market to move in a particular direction over time. The best way to describe a market trend is with a simple question: When canoeing in a river, is it easier to paddle with the current or against it? Trading is the same way. The collective will of traders forms the current. If good value is perceived in the market and traders want to bid prices higher, the trend (or current) is up. If traders perceive poor valuations and want to sell their shares, the trend (or current) is down.

It is impossible to make a living as a trader if you constantly fight the flow of the market. The odds of making successful trades increase when you are paddling with the current since overall market flows tend to affect individual equity prices. A good analogy for this concept is picturing yourself as a store manager inside the door of an electronics or department store on Black Friday (the day after Thanksgiving). Once that door opens, if you had any thoughts of going outside for something, forget it. The best thing to do is to move with the mob or to stand aside if the mob is moving in a direction you don't want to go.

Trends can be divided into three different durations. For example, in a daily time frame the following categories would be appropriate: short term (up to one month), intermediate term (one to three months), and long term (over three months). In a weekly time frame, these may be appropriate: short term (up to 8 weeks), intermediate term (8 to 26 weeks), and long term (over 26 weeks). There is no definitive set of values to identify trend lengths, but these are generally acceptable time frames for trend identification and classification. As a trader, you need to pick the trend duration that best fits your trading style. If you want to be more of an active trader, you may find the short end of the spectrum more appealing. If you would rather hold your positions for weeks or even months, the longer end of the trend range would apply.

Since trend is so important to making trading profits, let's take a look at three basic methods to identify the trend:

1. Pattern of highs and lows
2. Trendlines
3. Price moving averages

Pattern of Highs and Lows

Probably the simplest way to identify the trend of the market is to look at the pattern of highs and lows. In an *uptrend*, price makes higher highs and higher lows, whereas in a *downtrend*, price makes lower highs and lower lows. This simple trend identification technique brings up a very important point. Whenever you open a chart as a trader, the *first* thing you should take notice of is the price plot, not an indicator or even a candlestick line or pattern but the direction of the price action. Indicators can be out of sync with the price action, and many candlestick lines and patterns require traders to use some form of trend analysis to understand the context in which they appear. Price trend provides the initial foundation on which meaningful analysis is built.

The longer you plan to hold your positions, the more important the overall trend is to your trading results. Short-term trends tend to be much more volatile and change more quickly than longer-term trends; this means that short-term trends are best left to nimble, active traders. The daily chart of the SPDR Dow Jones Industrial Average ETF Trust in Figure 5-7 shows a long-term trend. Note the pattern of higher highs and higher lows as price advanced from July 2009 to January 2010.

Figure 5-7 provides an example of how a trend can be identified on a chart without the aid of indicators or deep analysis. One look tells a trader that the trend is up and that long trades should be given strong consideration.

Downtrends are a time to trade by executing short trades or simply standing aside and waiting for price to begin a new

FIGURE 5-7

Price Pattern in an Uptrend in SPDR Dow Jones Industrial
Average ETF Trust, Daily

Source: MetaStock

uptrend. Downtrends tend to be more volatile because they are
much more emotional events than uptrends. In uptrends, traders
are more sanguine with regard to market and news events, almost
to the point of complacency. In downtrends, the fear of a loss
drives traders to make rash decisions that can cause erratic market
movements. As a result of the elevated emotional level of downtrends, making consistent profits by short selling is much more
difficult than buying a position and holding it in an uptrend.
Downtrending markets should be approached with great care by
new traders. The daily chart of Cisco Systems in Figure 5-8 shows
a downtrend.

Trendlines

An additional tool to help with trend analysis is the *trendline*. A
trendline is a line that is drawn to connect at least two lows in

FIGURE 5-8

Price Pattern in a Downtrend for Cisco Systems, Daily

Source: MetaStock

an uptrend or at least two highs in a downtrend. Trendlines act as support or resistance that can give a trader a good price zone for making trading decisions. For example, if a trader is looking to add positions in an uptrend, waiting for price to pull back near the trendline may be a good idea. Conversely, an aggressive trader who wants to short the market may wait for price to move higher in the vicinity of a downsloping trendline. The discussion of trendlines can be quite complex, but for our purposes we will use simple examples to demonstrate how trendline analysis can help a trader in his or her decision-making process.

The daily chart of KLA-Tencor Corporation in Figure 5-9 shows how trendlines can be used not only to identify the trend but also to alert a trader to changes in the trend. The first thing to notice when looking at the chart is the lower price low made in June in relation to the previous low in May. That shows that a downtrend is in effect. Next, a downsloping trendline can be

FIGURE 5-9

Daily Trendlines for KLA-Tencor Corporation, Daily

Source: MetaStock

drawn connecting the highs beginning with the June 1 price high. Any traders looking to add long-side exposure would have been wise to wait for a break of that down trendline as an indication that buyers were returning to the market. After the hammer that was formed at point B, price reversed higher with a long white candle that broke the trendline. Price then rallied higher before pulling back and forming a spinning top on July 8. After that low, price once again reversed higher, which gave two points (price lows) to construct a short-term up trendline. By extending that line to the right, one can see that it gave an important support area for price as it rallied higher into August. As price pulled back in mid-August, the trendline drawn a month earlier provided solid support. Any traders looking to add to their positions in KLA-Tencor Corporation during that period could have used the price values around the trendline as a great place to execute a trade. One last note: Even though trendline support held in mid-August, there was trouble brewing on the right side of the chart. Notice how a shooting star formed just as price encountered resistance at the early August high. This shows that although support held and price appreciated from the trendline, a trader always must be on his or her toes to be constantly aware of ever-changing market conditions.

Trendlines are very effective in weekly time frames as well. The weekly chart of the Cohen & Steers Realty Majors ETF in Figure 5-10 gives an example of both short- and long-term trendlines and their ability to provide trade entry points for longer-term traders.

Note once again how price had been in a steep downtrend in the months before the March 2009 low. The first signal that a trend change was developing was the bullish engulfing pattern just past the low at point A. Price rallied sharply higher after that before pulling back in June 2009. The June–July pullback provided an opportunity to draw a short-term down trendline by connecting their tops. The spinning top followed by a long white

FIGURE 5-10

Weekly Trendlines for Cohen & Steers Realty Majors ETF, Weekly

Source: MetaStock

candle in July showed that buyers were reentering the market and that the ETF was ready to move higher once again. The July low also provided an opportunity to connect that low with the March low to draw a longer-term trendline (drawn from point A). After the break of trendline B, price rallied until it pulled back again in February 2010. The extension of the trendline that began at point A provided an idea where support could be expected in a pullback. Sure enough, price formed a hammer while it found support at the trendline. Price rallied again, breaking trendline C with a long white candle that gave traders an indication again that the uptrend was resuming. Trendlines in weekly time frames are great tools that give longer-term traders the ability to build positions over time.

Trendlines are great for managing trades in trending markets, but they also can be used to manage risk. Recall that Chapter 1 described how technical analysis can be used to manage risk and would have allowed traders virtually to sidestep the 2008 market meltdown. Now, using what we have just learned, let's take another look at Figure 1-3 by referring to Figure 5-11, which also shows the S&P 500. As price moved higher, it made a series of higher highs and higher lows from March 2003 to October 2007. That alone provided enough evidence that equities were in a strong uptrend, which provided a favorable environment for holding stocks. If one drew a trendline connecting the March 2003 low with the pullback low in the summer of 2006, a line in the sand would become evident as price moved higher. Any close below that line was a signal that continuation of the uptrend could be in jeopardy. Price pulled back and touched the trendline in August 2007 before rallying to its final high in October 2007. In December 2007, price came crashing down through the up trendline, signaling that the market trend was changing, which created an unfavorable environment for owning stocks. Whenever a long-term trendline (in this case four and a half years) is violated, it is a sign that major market changes are coming. The violation of this trendline in 2007 was a signal that the risk of loss to those holding stocks had increased. Anyone who failed to heed this simple yet important warning paid a very steep price as the market meltdown of 2008 was just beginning.

FIGURE 5-11

Trend Reversal in S&P 500 Index, Weekly

Source: MetaStock

Price Moving Averages

A price moving average shows the average price for a security over a specific time period. Moving averages are used to smooth price fluctuations and provide an indication of the price trend. A rising moving average reflects an uptrend in price, and a falling moving average reflects a downtrend in price. Moving averages come in many varieties, such as simple, exponential, weighted, volume-adjusted, and triangular. Some interesting things can be done with price moving averages, such as creating a price envelope by computing a moving average of high prices and a moving average of low prices.

A simple moving average is the easiest type to compute manually. This is done by adding up the last *n* days of closing prices and dividing by n. For example, to compute a 10-day simple moving average, add together the closing prices over the last 10 days and divide by 10. It is called a moving average because the average keeps moving forward as new data are added. When a new close is posted, that value is added to the data stream and the oldest day (in this case the eleventh day back) is dropped, and the most recent 10 days are averaged. The longer the duration of the moving average is, the smoother the moving average line will be. A shorter moving average will track much closer to actual price action and turn more quickly as price changes direction, but it also will appear more volatile and be less reliable if it is used to help determine the trend. Almost any competent charting software can display a moving average of price with a few simple mouse clicks. It is also important to note that whatever duration a moving average is, that duration is *trading* days, not *calendar* days. That means that a 10-day moving average is the same as a two-week moving average since there are five trading days in a week.

Moving averages are very flexible tools that can not only confirm a price trend but also provide support and resistance areas for price. Two of the most widely used moving averages in the investing world are the 50-day and 200-day moving averages. These particular moving averages are known as lines in the sand for intermediate (50 days) and long-term (200 days) trends. It is uncanny how many times price will find support or resistance at the 50- and 200-day moving averages. It is wise, however, to try moving averages of other durations that fit the time frame you choose to trade.

Whatever time frame or moving average type you choose, it is always important to observe how price behaves as it comes close to its moving average. Crosses above the moving average are seen as bullish, and crosses below are viewed as bearish. The daily chart of 3M Company in Figure 5-12 shows how price reacts to its own 40-day (intermediate-term) simple moving average, first in a downtrend and then in an uptrend.

Notice first how price reacted when encountering the moving average at points A and B on the chart. 3M was in an obvious downtrend as demonstrated by the price pattern of lower highs and lower lows along with a declining 40-day moving average. At point A, a shooting star was formed as price tried to break

FIGURE 5-12

Forty-Day Simple Moving Average for 3M Company, Daily

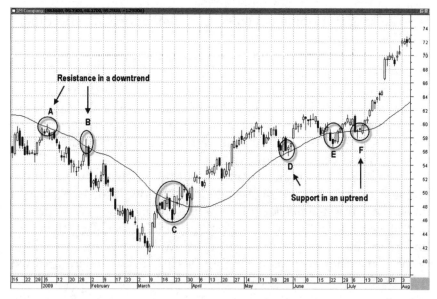

Source: MetaStock

through the moving average. When that attempt failed, price continued its decline. Price then rallied back up to point B, where another, more pronounced shooting star was formed; this showed a lack of resolve among buyers to push price through the moving average.

After the failure at point B, price declined further into its March 2009 low. A brief price bounce in March brought price right back to its 40-day moving average (point C). This time, price was able to break through the moving average briefly before forming two black candles as sellers took price below the moving average once again. The next day, however, a long white candle was formed to take price up through the moving average, where it paused for two days by forming an inverted hammer and a spinning top. After that brief period of indecision, another long white candle formed, which was a signal that buyers were assuming control of the trend. Price moved higher from there, beginning a new uptrend. An important point to emphasize here is that the 40-day moving average did not begin to move higher until mid-April even though price actually bottomed in early March. This is known as a *lag*. The longer a moving average is, the more of a lag effect there is to confirm changes in trend.

Once the new uptrend was started, there were three points where price interacted with the moving average as both price and the moving average moved higher. Notice at points D and F how the candles formed tails or long lower shadows as selling pressure diminished as price encountered the moving average. In both instances at points D and F, the candles formed hammers, after which price reversed and moved higher.

Point E was an interesting situation in that price actually violated the moving average as it closed below it for two straight days. After the two black candles, a long white candle was formed that closed above the moving average, quickly negating the cross lower. In this case, the price close below the moving average at point E was not seen as a terribly bearish event. There are two reasons for that. First, price was below the moving average for only two days before quickly crossing back above it. Second, the moving average itself was still moving higher, signaling upward price momentum. Although crosses above and below moving averages are always worth noting, not all should be viewed as potential game changers.

Since moving averages act as support and resistance, it is also possible to use them as confirmations that short-term trend reversals have indeed taken place. The example of SanDisk Corporation in Figure 5-13 uses a 13-period exponential moving average. Exponential moving averages give more weight to recent prices, which makes them more sensitive to recent price activity. This differs from the simple moving average method, which gives each value equal weight over the chosen time period. Exponential moving averages (EMAs) are computed by applying a percentage of the most recent closing price to the previous moving average value. The percentage value used on the EMA can be converted to time periods, which is what most traders prefer. Almost any competent software package will allow a trader to plot an exponential moving average with a couple of mouse clicks, and so I will not go into the conversion of the percentage value to days in the EMA.

FIGURE 5-13

Thirteen-Day Exponential Moving Average for SanDisk
Corporation, Daily

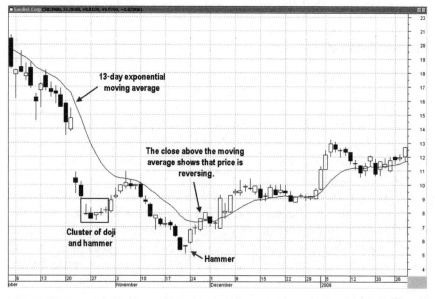

Source: MetaStock

Steven Achelis does a splendid job of explaining the calculation
and conversion of values from percentages to time periods in exponential moving averages in his book *Technical Analysis from A to Z.*

Notice how price moves lower on the left side of the chart,
staying below the moving average before forming a cluster of
candles that have reversal implications. In the boxed area, three doji
and one hammer were formed. That candle cluster was followed
by a four-day advance that ran smack into resistance at the moving
average before reversing lower to continue the downtrend. Unless
you are an active trader who takes positions off after a few days,
this would not have been a good trade to take. The move lower
continued until a hammer was formed, followed by a long white
candle at the bottom of the chart. Although this was a valid
reversal signal, waiting for further confirmation on a close above
the moving average was the prudent thing to do for those looking
for a longer-term trade. Again, the moving average was looming

overhead and would act as resistance. Two days later, price closed above the moving average, providing confirmation that a trend change was very likely. After a brief pullback, price continued higher, proving that the price trend had indeed changed.

SUMMARY

Support and resistance are two concepts that lend more weight to candlestick lines and patterns. Reversal patterns (Chapter 3) that form at support or resistance levels have a higher chance for success, and continuation patterns (Chapter 4) that break through the same levels show the strength of trends. Support and resistance come in the form of prior highs and lows, retracements, trendlines, and moving averages.

Trading in the direction of the market trend gives a trader a chance to harness the energy of the market, which increases the chance of trading success. Price pattern analysis, trendlines, and moving averages are three methods that can be used to identify and trade with the overall trend. Entering trades without being aware of the market trend can leave a trader open to devastating losses. When opening a price chart, the first thing to do (before looking for candlestick lines and patterns) is to identify the direction of price movement. Just like paddling a canoe, moving with the current (the flow of the market) is much easier than moving against it.

CHAPTER 6

Candlesticks and Momentum Indicators

As has been demonstrated in Chapters 1–5, candlesticks can provide much more depth of information than other charting methodologies can. This chapter will add another layer to our analysis by including *momentum indicators*. A momentum indicator is used to measure the *rate* at which price moves up or down. Momentum indicators are flexible in that they can be computed over any time frame to provide a short-, intermediate-, or long-term view of price movement. When coupled with candlestick charting, these indicators can reinforce candlestick lines or patterns that develop in the price plot.

A word of caution is in order, however. If you are new to momentum indicators, it is very easy to become enamored with these indicators that open up a whole new world of price movement analysis. Many traders who are using these indicators for the first time tend to rely on them too heavily for trading decisions, and that can lead to unnecessary losses. In trading the markets, it is always best to employ a *weight of the evidence* methodology, which simply means that signals or patterns must confirm each other before one enters a trade. Momentum indicators are used to measure the health of the trend in the momentum of price movement, not the actual trend in price movement. This means that if a shift in *price momentum* is developing, *price itself* must confirm the momentum signal with a change in direction. Remember that technical analysis is used not to make hard and fast predictions but to tilt the odds of success more firmly in your favor before you execute a trade.

Momentum indicators have different properties and different looks, but when all is said and done, they generally serve the same purpose in analyzing the market. The three main uses of momentum indicators are

1. Displaying overbought and oversold levels—or levels from which price momentum is likely to slow or change direction.
2. Revealing divergences between price movement and its momentum.
3. Analyzing the momentum trend.

The momentum indicators presented in this chapter are all forms of oscillators in that they oscillate either between overbought and oversold levels (banded oscillators) or above and below a centerline (centered oscillators). Regardless of the classification of any particular momentum indicator, remember that all are used for basically the three main purposes listed above. Also, when one is using momentum indicators for overbought/oversold levels, the longer the time period being computed is, the *smoother* the indicator will be, which means it is less likely to reach the same overbought and oversold levels as shorter time frames. This will become apparent as you spend time experimenting with momentum indicators of differing time lengths. The examples given here are meant to serve as a foundation for combining these indicators with candlesticks. It will be up to you to take your analysis further and be creative in developing a trading style that fits your personality.

MOVING AVERAGE OSCILLATOR

A *moving average oscillator* is simply the difference between a shorter- and a longer-term price moving average (moving averages were discussed in Chapter 5). This concept is the basis for the moving average convergence/divergence (MACD) indicator that will be examined later in this chapter, but for now let's take a look at a simple oscillator that can be of great use in analyzing price movement.

A moving average oscillator is computed by subtracting the longer-term moving average from the shorter-term moving average. This generates a centered oscillator that moves above and below a zero line. When the oscillator is above the zero line, the shorter-term moving average is above the longer-term moving average, which is positive for price momentum. When the oscillator is below the zero line, the shorter-term moving average is below the longer-term moving average, which is negative for price momentum.

The daily chart of Apple Inc. in Figure 6-1 illustrates the use of a moving average oscillator. In this case the oscillator is constructed by subtracting a 20-day exponential moving average (EMA) from a 5-day EMA. This is a good combination to use as it encompasses a short-term time frame (5 days) and a time frame that is on the cusp between short and intermediate time frames (20 days = 1 month of trading).

FIGURE 6-1

Moving Average Oscillator for Apple Inc., Daily

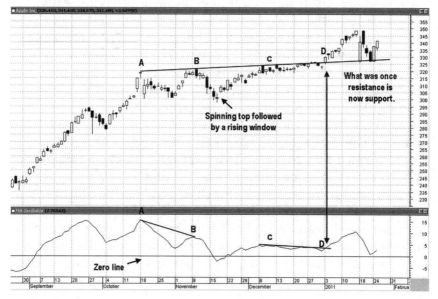

Source: MetaStock

The first point of reference is the difference between price and the oscillator from point A to point B. As price made a higher high from A to B, the oscillator made a lower high at point B. This is an example of a *negative divergence,* which occurs when price pushes out to a higher high but the oscillator makes a lower high. The negative divergence was a signal that upward price momentum (or velocity) was decreasing. Notice that at the negative divergence at point B, a bearish engulfing pattern was formed. This is more weight of the evidence that a decline was likely to unfold. Price declined for six days before forming a short-term low consisting of a spinning top followed by a rising window, which started another push higher. The benefit of charts like this is that the resistance line is obvious, but in real-time trading at the time the divergence formed at point B, there was no resistance *line* yet, only the one time resistance formed by the reversal lower at point A. After price declined off point B, that presented an opportunity to connect points A and B and extend the line to the right to use as a resistance line in the future.

After the short-term low, price rebounded and once again encountered the resistance line at point C. Comparing the action just after price encountered the resistance line at point C with its encounter at point B shows a change in price behavior. Although price declined rather sharply after point B, it continued to touch the resistance line and move sideways after point C. The fact that price did not decline noticeably after encountering the resistance line was a sign that the resistance line was weakening and that a breakout above the line was becoming probable. The oscillator (in the lower pane on the chart) after point C mimicked the price behavior as it was being held in check by its own resistance line drawn from point C. The white candle breakout over resistance at point D was confirmed by a breakout over resistance in the oscillator that showed that upside momentum was building once again.

The final point regarding this chart involves the principle that what was once resistance is now support (see Chapter 5). Note that as price moved to a new high after the breakout over resistance, it pulled back and found support on the extended line that was once resistance at points A, B, and C. Price bounced off that line twice as it consolidated in the range of 330 to 350.

The next example makes use of shorter-term moving averages. The daily chart of JPMorgan Chase in Figure 6-2 uses a 3/10-day EMA oscillator. This example once again shows the power of divergences along with candlestick patterns to alert a trader that a change in price direction is near.

First, notice that price moved higher along the resistance line from point A to point B to point C. The moving average oscillator confirmed the price movement from point A to point B but failed miserably at point C, which was an indication that the push higher in price was losing steam. At point C, a bearish candlestick pattern was forming (circled) that included a bearish harami and a hanging man. Once price broke lower out of this pattern, a short trade could have been taken with a higher level of confidence because of the loss of upside momentum as demonstrated by the moving average oscillator.

FIGURE 6-2

Moving Average Oscillator for JPMorgan Chase, Daily

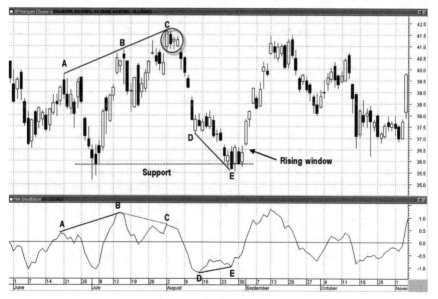

Source: MetaStock

After the reversal at point C, price broke down sharply, forming lows at point D and point E. Price found support at point E as it encountered a prior low made in the range of 35.50 to 36 (dashed line). The big question here was, would price consolidate and continue lower as it had at point D, or would buyers step in at this level and drive the price higher? The moving average oscillator gave a clue to what price was likely to do. Note that as price declined from point D to point E, the oscillator made a higher low, forming a *positive divergence*. This occurs when price makes a lower low but the oscillator makes a higher low. The cluster of candles at E as support held showed that buyers were putting the brakes on the decline and a battle over short-term direction was developing. A rising window was formed as price broke up out of the cluster at point E, showing that the buyers had won the battle.

Although divergences are great ways to flag decreasing price momentum, trading too soon on these signals alone can prove costly to a trader's account. A divergence is a signal that shows only that the velocity of price movement is slowing. Think of it as driving a car at a constant speed. If you remove your foot from the gas pedal, the car does not immediately go into reverse; it simply moves in the same direction at a slower rate of speed. In much the same way, divergences between price and momentum indicators can last for days. Just as with candlestick reversal patterns, wait for price to confirm a reversal before initiating a trade.

RATE OF CHANGE

Rate of change is very easy to calculate and is an effective indicator. The simple method of calculation is misleading to those who believe that the more complex the formula behind an indicator is, the more effective the indicator is. Rate of change is an indicator that is elegant in its simplicity, yet it opens up an extra dimension in the analysis of price movement.

Rate of change (ROC) is simply the difference between today's closing price and the closing price n periods ago. There are two ways to calculate rate of change. The first is subtraction: $ROC = C - Cn$, where C is today's closing price and Cn is the close price n periods ago.

The second method (the one I prefer) is the division method: $ROC = [(C/Cn) - 1] \times 100$, where C is today's closing price and Cn

is the closing price n periods ago. The division method provides a more realistic look at how much price actually changed on a percentage basis. For example, consider the different methods of computation in a $2 move higher between a $5 and a $50 stock. Using the subtraction method, a $2 move in either stock would yield a result of 2 in both cases (the difference between the current price and the price n periods ago). When the division method is used, the results would be 40 for the lower-priced stock (a 40 percent move) and 4 for the higher priced stock (a 4 percent move). The division method shows the impact a price move can have on stocks that are priced at different levels.

Since rate of change is a centered oscillator, readings above the zero line demonstrate positive price momentum and readings below zero represent negative price momentum. Just as with any momentum indicator, one of its strengths is its ability to show momentum divergences from price. The daily chart of JPMorgan Chase in Figure 6-3 shows multiple divergences over a two-month

FIGURE 6-3

Price Rate of Change for JPMorgan Chase, Daily

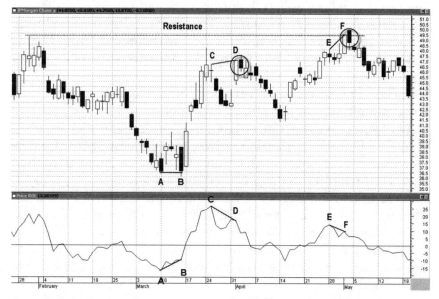

Source: MetaStock

time frame using a 10-day price rate of change. Combining these divergences with candlestick analysis gives a trader a deeper look into price movement and lends a higher degree of confidence to any trading decisions that are made.

Notice the price action at the March low on the chart between points A and B. Price at point B came down to the same point where support was found at point A. Now take a look at the 10-day ROC at the bottom of the chart. The ROC actually rose between points A and B. This is technically not a divergence per se, because price did not make a lower low while the ROC made a higher low, but it is enough of a difference between the two to show latent positive momentum building in JPMorgan Chase at the March low. The large white candle that formed the day after point B was an indication that positive momentum was taking price higher.

Next, take a look at points C and D on the price plot and on the rate of change plot at the bottom of the chart. This was an all-out negative divergence as price pushed to a higher high from C to D while the rate of change indicator made a lower high. The black candle at point D (circled) was more of a thrusting line than a dark cloud cover because its close did not penetrate at least halfway into the real body of the previous white candle. When coupled with the negative divergence in the ROC, however, it was an ominous sign. The fact that it occurred at the prior high made at point C showed a short-term failure at resistance. The dark candle combined with the evident drop in momentum (negative divergence from C to D on the ROC indicator) showed that the odds were increasing for a pullback.

The same situation occurred at points E and F, but this time it had more lasting implications. First, notice how as price pushed higher from E to F, the same divergence was present that occurred from C to D (higher price, lower ROC). Also notice that price was now in the same range as the high made in late January (dashed line). The final piece in this weight of the evidence scenario is again a failure at resistance as a black candle formed at point F (circled). Although the black candle's close may not have penetrated at least halfway into the real body of the previous white candle to generate a textbook dark cloud cover, there is enough evidence present to take the short trade once price closed below the real body of the black candle.

Other strengths of the rate of change indicator are that it is very good at showing overbought/oversold conditions and also at showing momentum trends, which can differ from price trends. Look at the daily chart of JPMorgan Chase in Figure 6-4, using a 10-day rate of change indicator.

Note the position of the rate of change indicator as price makes higher highs at points A, B, and C. The rate of change peaks at around 10 and turns lower in each case. These momentum turning points coincide with short-term price tops as reflected by the loss of upward price momentum. The upper line drawn over the rate of change indicator at around the value of 10 is the overbought line. In other words, every time the rate of change indicator reaches this level, a decrease in momentum and a short-term change in price direction are likely. This does not mean that a reversal of some sort is *guaranteed*; it is merely a warning that a short-term change in momentum and possibly price direction *could* occur. Also note how as price bottoms before point B, the rate of

FIGURE 6-4

Price Rate of Change for JPMorgan Chase, Daily

Source: MetaStock

change touched the bottom or oversold line at around –7. Again, this was an indication of a *possible* change in momentum and price direction. Notice the trading opportunities that presented themselves at points B and C. In each case, the ROC was in overbought territory while reversal candle lines were formed at point B (doji) and point C (spinning top/harami). The weight of the evidence was showing that a pullback in price was due, and that presented great opportunities for aggressive short-term traders.

Overbought and oversold levels can change or shift depending on the trend. In uptrending markets, overbought and oversold levels tend to be higher than they are in downtrending markets. A great example is shown in Figure 6-4. Notice how after point B on the chart the ROC tends to bottom at or near the zero line. That shows strong upward momentum. In strong downtrends, the overbought area is likely to be found at or near the zero line. This is why it is so important to be cognizant of the market trend in the time frame in which you plan to trade.

The next point with regard to Figure 6-4 is how the rate of change indicator also showed an uptrend along with price in December and early January. The ROC made a series of higher lows, which showed positive momentum. Using a trendline on a momentum indicator can reveal when momentum is waning, as it did in early January. Notice how price chopped sideways with a collection of spinning tops and longer upper shadows after the momentum trendline was broken. This lack of short-term direction was preceded by the trendline break in the rate of change indicator.

Thus far the examples presented have looked at the short term. The rate of change indicator also can be used in much longer-term time frames to provide a much longer look at the condition of the markets. This example uses the weekly chart of the S&P 500 in Figure 6-5 and takes a closer look at the 2007 market top.

This version of the chart, which has been presented previously in Figures 1-3 and 5-11, zeros in a bit closer on the October 2007 top. Price is plotted in the top window, with a 40-week rate of change plotted in the bottom window. These longer-term views can warn a trader that storm clouds are gathering on the horizon with regard to the major market trend. Recall that one of the benefits of technical analysis is that it alerts traders when the level of risk is rising in the market.

FIGURE 6-5

Forty-Week Price Rate of Change for S&P 500 Index, Weekly

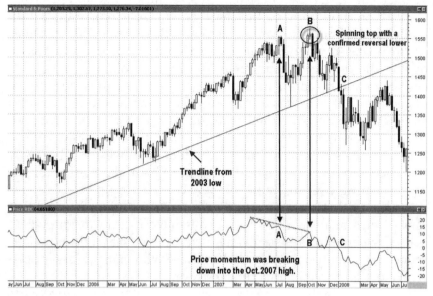

Source: MetaStock

First, take a look at points A and B on the chart. As price made a higher high from point A to point B, the 40-week rate of change made a lower high, which formed a negative divergence. The weight of the evidence was enhanced by the spinning top that was formed at point B, followed immediately by a long black candle, which confirmed a price reversal. The momentum drop with the candlestick reversal showed that the long-term uptrend from March 2003 was in serious jeopardy of reversing lower. The final piece of evidence that the uptrend was over came at point C. Notice at point C how price broke its 4.5-year trendline while at the same time the 40-week ROC slipped below zero, signaling negative momentum for the market. Also notice that after the trendline break, a spinning top was formed, which showed brief indecision among traders. Another long black candle formed the next week, which confirmed that the uptrend was indeed over and that a more defensive posture must be assumed.

One other piece of valuable analysis can be seen by looking at the entire price plot on the chart. Notice how the candle lines are smaller yet somewhat consistent in size during the uptrend from the 2005 starting point on the chart. Now take a look at the length of the candle lines between points A and B. The longer candle lines show increased volatility, which is a characteristic that was absent during the bulk of the uptrend. The higher volatility signaled a change in trader sentiment as buyers and sellers battled for control of the trend. It was also a form of exhaustion as the final buyers rushed in to make sure they didn't miss any more of the uptrend. This is a characteristic that trends exhibit before they reverse course as the sanguine attitude of traders and investors gives way to a final shot of greed as traders want to be in the market for the next, seemingly certain move higher. This change in behavior was another clue that a trend change was on the way. Keep in mind that longer-term analysis does not always have to lead to immediate action as sometimes these events take time to play out; however, longer-term analysis can be used by those who manage larger portfolios to adjust overall market exposure.

Rate of change is a very versatile indicator that can provide good analysis across any time frame. It has many uses not only with price but with other indicators as well. I encourage you to see how many different uses you can get out of this simple yet effective momentum indicator.

STOCHASTIC OSCILLATOR

A *stochastic oscillator* shows where the latest close is in relation to the price range over the desired period. It was introduced by George Lane and is a favorite among many traders because of its standardized scale and easy to follow signals.

The theory behind the stochastic oscillator is based on the premise that price closes closer to the upper end of its trading range in an uptrending market and closes nearer to the bottom of its trading range in a downtrending market. As price trends mature, closes near the extreme of the period become less common, alerting a trader that a change in trend may be imminent.

Construction of the stochastic consists of two oscillators called %K and %D. The data needed for %K are the current close along with the highest and lowest prices for the period being used. For example, in constructing a five-period %K, the current close, the highest high for the last five periods, and the lowest low for the last five periods would be used. The formula is as follows: %K = $100 \times [(C - Ln)/(Hn - Ln)]$, where Ln is the lowest low over the last n periods and Hn is the highest high over the last n periods. %D is a smoothed version of %K. Its calculation equates to a moving average of %K values. %D is typically a three-period smoothed version of %K, especially in shorter-term time frames, but it is perfectly acceptable to set one's own %D length.

In many charting packages, the stochastic oscillator that is used is referred to as a *slow stochastic*. A slow stochastic is a smoothed version of %K (the usual default is three periods), with a %D that is usually a three-period smoothing of the already smoothed %K. The setting for a five-period slow stochastic would be 5, 3, 3 with the 5 representing the number of periods used in the %K calculation, the first 3 representing the smoothing of %K (three periods), and the second 3 representing the smoothing of the smoothed %K line that yields the %D (also three periods). Thus, in effect, the %D in a slow stochastic is a double-smoothed version of the original %K. The reason for using the slow stochastic is that it is less volatile and gives more reliable trading signals than does the raw version of %K. The stochastic examples below all use the slow stochastic.

The stochastic is known as a *banded oscillator* because it has set levels that denote overbought and oversold momentum levels. The default values are 80 for overbought and 20 for oversold. In many cases, however, the range for overbought and oversold levels tends to shift, depending on the market trend. Also, the crossover of %K and %D is used by many as a timing signal for market entry and/or exit, but these crossover signals also can provide *whipsaw* signals, or rapid signals that switch from one direction to another over a short period. The examples below will reference the %K line (the solid line) when referring to the stochastic oscillator.

The daily chart of Microsoft Corporation in Figure 6-6 with a five-day stochastic oscillator (5, 3, 3) shows overbought/oversold levels, a negative divergence, and the way the range shifts as a trend develops and gains strength. First, note at points A, B, and D how the stochastic bottoms below 20 before turning higher. This shows that momentum has ebbed to the point where a rebound

FIGURE 6-6

Five-Day Stochastic Oscillator for Microsoft Corporation, Daily

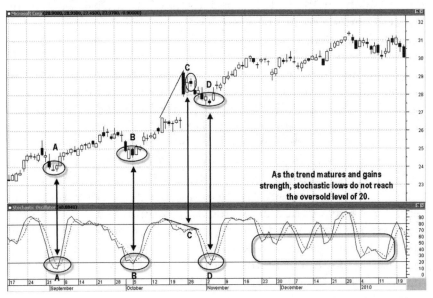

As the trend matures and gains strength, stochastic lows do not reach the oversold level of 20.

Source: MetaStock

is likely as price has closed near the bottom of its five-day range. Even when the stochastic reaches oversold territory, there is no guarantee that a rebound will occur. Bear in mind that when a market is oversold, it is simply a sign that the market has been weak over the time frame used in the stochastic, but it can get even weaker. To increase the odds of getting a good read on what price is likely to do, let's use the weight of the evidence methodology and see what the candlesticks are telling us.

At point A, as the stochastic bottomed below 20, notice that an inverted hammer appeared in the price plot that was followed by two white candles, signifying that a reversal in price was under way. The stochastic then crossed up over the 20 level to show that upward momentum was building. At point B, a bullish belt hold line developed that ultimately led to a reversal higher. Note how the stochastic climbed out of oversold territory at point B as a white candle was formed, giving the rise in momentum more credibility. Finally, at point D note how price formed two straight spinning tops (circled) as the stochastic dipped below 20. Once again, price reversed higher, confirming that upside momentum was building after the formation of the reversal candles.

Point C on the chart is another example of a momentum indicator giving a divergence. In this case a negative divergence was formed as price moved sharply higher on a rising window, yet the stochastic made a lower high. This divergence coincided with the formation of a spinning top (circled) that showed trader indecision. A reversal followed that took price lower into point D.

Another point to note is the range shift that was mentioned earlier. As the uptrend developed and strengthened, note how the lows in the stochastic never even reached 20 before price reversed higher. That activity showed that price was closing continually near the top of its five-day range, which is a sign of a strong trend. This is an example of knowing the characteristics of the indicator with which one is working.

The daily chart of Amazon.com in Figure 6-7 shows the trending characteristics of the stochastic oscillator. In this case a 10-day slow stochastic (10, 3, 3) is used. After price bottomed at the lower left of the chart in September 2009, the stochastic made a series of higher lows, which are connected with a trendline. This is a case of the momentum trend confirming the price trend. As price moved sharply higher into point A, a shooting star was formed (circled) that led to a price reversal. Once price reversed lower, momentum reversed with it as price and momentum each confirmed the decline of the other.

After the decline from point A, price rebounded briefly before starting another decline into point B. Look again at the stochastic as a trendline was drawn connecting the rebound high in December with a lower high formed in late January, verifying that momentum was trending lower along with price. At point B (circled), the price decline leveled off as strong support developed at the 115 price level. Notice at point B how many long-tailed candles (hammers and doji) formed. About halfway through the consolidation phase at point B, momentum had broken its downtrend line and had begun to move higher. This was an indication that upward momentum was building. The long white candle that formed to break out of the point B consolidation range was a sign that a new uptrend was beginning.

FIGURE 6-7

Ten-Day Stochastic Oscillator for Amazon.com, Daily

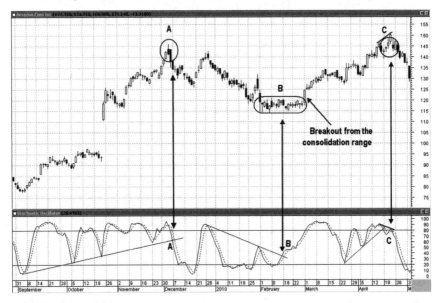

Source: MetaStock

Finally, take a look at the March low in the stochastic as it once again confirmed the uptrend in price with an uptrend of its own. As price approached the high at point C, notice how not only did a negative divergence form as price made a higher high and the stochastic made a lower high, the uptrend in momentum was violated as well. Also, as price made its final push into the high at point C (circled), the move contained a hanging man and a spinning top, hardly a display of conviction among buyers. At point C, the weight of the evidence (a hanging man and a spinning top, a momentum trend break, and a negative divergence) indicated that a reversal lower was near. A number of black candles formed that took price lower, confirming the reversal.

MACD

The moving average convergence/divergence (MACD) was created by Gerald Appel, and its name is derived from the fact that it is constructed of two separate moving averages that are either converging with or diverging from each other. The MACD is constructed by using one shorter and one longer exponential moving average (EMA). The default settings in charting packages such as MetaStock are 12 for the shorter-term EMA and 26 for the longer-term EMA. The difference between the shorter- and longer-term moving averages is plotted as a single line. The examples below use the typical default values (12 and 26). Feel free to experiment to see what combination of moving averages works best for you.

The MACD is a centered oscillator in that it contains a center, or zero, line. Readings above the zero line mean that the shorter-term moving average is above the longer-term moving average; readings below the zero line mean that the shorter-term moving average is below the longer-term moving average. The MACD typically is plotted with a *signal line,* which is usually defaulted to a 9 period EMA. Although many traders use crossovers of the signal line for buy and sell signals, this method is prone to whipsaw signals during trend changes which can reduce its reliability. More important, the MACD can show longer-term divergences of the price trend that provide advance signals that a change in trend may be developing.

Because the MACD trends well, it lends itself to longer-term market analysis. For this example, we will look at the S&P 500 weekly in Figure 6-8 to show that the MACD could have been used to confirm that at the very least a top of some sort was forming in October 2007. After the April 2005 low at the left side of the chart, the MACD confirmed the uptrend in price as it also made higher highs while finding support at the zero line all the way up to point A in June 2007. This confirmation showed that the trend was strong and sustainable. After point A, however, the MACD began to diverge from price. As price made a higher high from point A to point B, the MACD made a lower high. This was a short-term divergence (from a weekly perspective), which indicated that the push to the high at B had gotten ahead of itself and that a pullback was due. That pullback came in the form of a very sharp correction into August before the final push higher into point C.

While price was making higher highs from A to B to C on the chart, the MACD was making a series of lower highs, showing a decline in price momentum. In other words, the push necessary to

FIGURE 6-8

MACD for S&P 500, Weekly

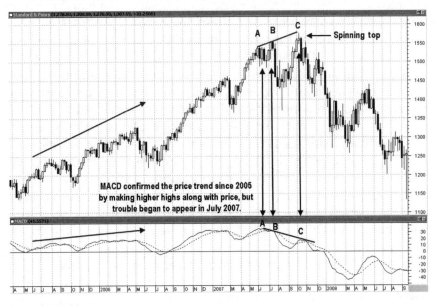

Source: MetaStock

sustain higher prices was no longer present. The nonconfirmation by the MACD gave the spinning top formed in October 2007 much more weight as a valid reversal signal. The advance warning from the MACD coupled with the spinning top gave longer-term position traders and portfolio managers plenty of time to adjust their positions before the 2008 meltdown gained full steam. This type of analysis can allow traders to stay a step ahead of the market by reducing their exposure as market conditions change. In this sense technical analysis helps traders and even long-term investors manage risk by heeding the storm clouds gathering on the horizon.

Was there any way a trader could have known how deep the reversal was going to go once the spinning top reversal was confirmed in October 2007? Not really. However, there is one indication that can provide insight that will let a trader know when a divergence is ready to lead to something deeper than the average garden-variety pullback. Notice how long the negative divergence lasted from point A to point C on the chart as momentum deteriorated while price made new highs. That type of action shows cracks in the foundation of the rally over a time span of four months. Typically, the longer and more pronounced the divergence is, the more severe the pullback will be.

Let's take a look at the MACD in a daily time frame to show how its trending characteristics can be used to alert a trader when a change in market direction is likely. The daily chart of Google in Figure 6-9 demonstrates the use of a trendline on the MACD. The chart begins in October 2006 as price formed a rising window and made a reactionary high at point A. Price pulled back and rallied once again, pushing out to a higher high at point B, where a spinning top reversal was formed. While price formed a higher high at B, the MACD made a lower high. Price then declined before once again charging higher into point C, as the MACD declined further, beginning a momentum downtrend. That downtrend continued until March 2007, when the MACD broke its downtrend

FIGURE 6-9

MACD for Google, Daily

Source: MetaStock

line as two long white candles formed. The March breakout was a signal that upside momentum was gaining strength as buyers reentered the market.

The strength of the MACD lies in its trending qualities, which make it a great tool for longer-term momentum analysis. Its smooth plot encourages the use of trendlines that when violated can give a trader advance warning of a probable change in price direction.

RELATIVE STRENGTH INDEX

The *Relative Strength Index* (RSI) was introduced by J. Welles Wilder in 1978. This indicator measures price momentum only and should not be confused with relative strength comparisons from one security to another. The strength of the RSI lies in its calculation, which includes data from every day over the period being computed; that makes it a more robust indicator than some of its momentum counterparts. For example, a 14-day RSI contains data from each day over the 14-day period. Contrast that with the rate of change indicator, which compares only two data points (today's close and the close n periods ago), or the stochastic, which uses today's close and the highest high and lowest low of the period. The RSI is computed as follows: $RSI = 100 \times [100/(1 + RS)]$, where RS is the average of up days over the period divided by the average of down days over the period.

Since the RSI uses the averages of up and down days, it is less affected by sharp price moves than is the ROC or the stochastic. The RSI is a banded oscillator, which means that it has fixed levels that are considered overbought and oversold. The standard default values for these levels are 70 (overbought) and 30 (oversold). The longer the period used to compute the RSI is (28 days, for example), the shallower the momentum swings will be. For this reason, the overbought and oversold levels should be adjusted for volatility. Typically, the longer the time frame that is used, the less volatile the indicator readings will be. For example, a five-day (one-week) RSI may work better with overbought/oversold levels of 80/20, whereas a 14-day RSI would work better with the standard 70/30 levels. A trader also must be mindful of the trend when using overbought and oversold levels. For example, in an uptrend, a 14-day

RSI tends to bottom in the range of 40 to 50, rarely reaching the standard oversold level of 30. In a downtrend, the 14-day RSI tends to top in the range of 50 to 60, rarely reaching the standard over-bought level of 70. Learning the tendencies of the RSI and com-bining them with candlestick analysis allows a trader to create a very stable trading methodology.

The daily chart of the PowerShares QQQ Trust ETF in Fig-ure 6-10 shows how combining a 14-day RSI with candlesticks can present opportunities to add positions in an uptrend. Recall that in trending markets the range of overbought and oversold tends to shift. The chart shows that this ETF was clearly in an uptrend as it made higher highs and higher lows in the second half of 2009. The RSI also reflected the uptrend by bottoming well above the standard oversold level of 30 (the dashed line at the bottom of the RSI window). The shaded area is where the 14-day RSI is expected to bottom in an uptrend (40–50).

FIGURE 6-10

RSI for PowerShares QQQ Trust ETF, Daily

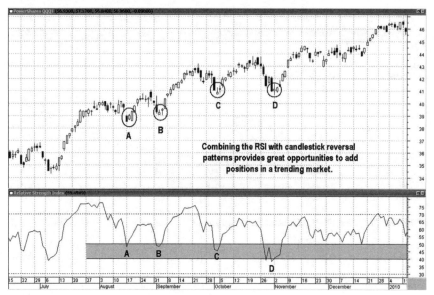

Source: MetaStock

In each case, as the RSI fell into the oversold zone for an uptrend, the candlestick pattern showed reversal characteristics. At point A, a reversal was formed by a long white candle as the uptrend resumed. Point B had two reversal candlesticks (inverted hammer and hammer) as the RSI was below 50. Point C had an inverted hammer and a spinning top as the RSI pulled back to 45. Point D formed a spinning top as the RSI bottomed in the 40 area. This weight of the evidence approach can allow a trader to add risk exposure at reasonable levels during an uptrend without having to chase the market.

The RSI lends itself to the use of trendlines to get a measure of the price momentum trend and its likelihood of continuing. Trendline violations can alert a trader that latent buying or selling pressure is developing. The daily chart of Intel Corporation in Figure 6-11 illustrates the use of trendlines in detecting a shift in price momentum. Intel had begun a downtrend after the May 6, 2010, flash crash. The period shown begins in June 2010. The

FIGURE 6-11

RSI for Intel Corporation, Daily

Source: MetaStock

principle of range shift is used in this example, only this time it shows where the RSI tends to top in downtrends. The shaded area is the range of 50 to 60, which is a place where a trader should look for a reversal lower in a downtrend.

As price topped in July (point A), three straight hanging man candles were formed, which showed indecision as the move higher in price had stalled while the RSI was at the 60 level. Price then broke lower, confirmed by the downtrend in momentum as shown by the downsloping momentum trendline drawn from point A to point B in the lower window. At point B, the RSI broke above its down trendline, showing that price momentum may have been shifting. Remember, though, that the fact that the momentum trend may be changing is no reason to jump in and buy without some form of confirmation by price. Price very well can continue to go lower while momentum continues to diverge. The momentum shift is merely a signal to be alert for a confirmed change in price direction.

If an aggressive trader had purchased on the initial white candle off the low formed at point B, the stop should have been placed below the low of point B. A more conservative method would have been to wait for a violation of the price trendline to confirm the violation of the downtrend in momentum. Also, some form of candle that confirmed that downward pressure was indeed abating would stack the weight of the evidence even more in the trader's favor. That candle came at point C in the form of a doji as price approached the previous low at point B. The next day, the downtrend line in price was violated by a rising window and a long white candle, which showed that a change in price trend was under way. Waiting for the doji in this case would have provided a slightly less desirable trade entry price, but in many cases waiting for confirmation of a trend change requires sacrificing what later turns out to be the optimal entry point.

SUMMARY

Momentum indicators are valuable technical analysis tools that measure the velocity of price movement. Their confirmation of or divergence from price activity alerts traders when a trend is in good health or is likely to slow and possibly reverse. When they are combined with candlestick patterns, their ability to show trend continuations or reversals is enhanced. Each of the indicators shown in this chapter is a simple yet effective method to measure price momentum.

The moving average oscillator is the difference between two moving averages that can show divergences in momentum versus price movement and indicate whether the moving average configuration is positive or negative by its position relative to its zero line.

Rate of change is an indicator that compares where price is now with where it was n periods ago. Don't be fooled by its simple calculation as it is a very effective indicator for showing momentum trends and momentum trend divergences with price action.

A stochastic is a classic indicator that uses three data points in its calculation: the current close, the highest high, and the lowest low for the period. Although the crossover of the %K and %D lines sometimes is used for buy and sell signals, these crossovers can provide whipsaw signals during volatile markets. The stochastic is very effective in showing the momentum trend as well as revealing opportune times to add positions in the direction of an existing trend.

MACD is a smoother indicator that is great for measuring the momentum trend. Although some traders like to use the crossovers of its signal line as buy and sell signals, I am not a fan of that method because in more volatile conditions the MACD can provide errant crossover signals. The strength of the MACD lies in its ability to confirm longer-term price trends along with the use of trendlines to detect shifts in longer-term price momentum.

The RSI is one of my personal favorites because it takes into account every day of the period being calculated and thus is a more robust indicator. Do not confuse this indicator with relative strength comparisons between securities or between securities and the broader market. The RSI is a good choice not only for adding to positions in the direction of the existing price trend but also for showing the condition of the momentum trend.

In each case, be careful when using these indicators to measure overbought and/or oversold conditions because of the range shifts that occur in trending markets. In uptrends, momentum indicators tend to make higher highs and shallower lows, whereas in downtrending markets they tend to make lower highs and deeper lows.

This means that some flexibility is required to use them effectively, depending on the market conditions.

Momentum indicators have many other uses that were not covered in this chapter, such as smoothing the RSI or the rate of change with a moving average, pairing each indicator with its own moving average, and setting up multiple momentum indicators that cover different time frames on the same price plot. I strongly encourage anyone who wants to explore momentum indicators more deeply to read *Martin Pring on Market Momentum.* In my opinion, this is one of the best books ever written on price momentum indicators.

Don't ever be afraid to think outside the box with these indicators. It is always wise to understand how each indicator is constructed and what its basic uses are. However, limiting yourself to using them only one way or with a certain set of parameters will not expand your knowledge. By experimenting with them you can open up a whole new world of understanding regarding these indicators and their applications.

CHAPTER 7

Candlesticks
and Volume

Volume is a very important tool to use in market analysis, yet it often is overlooked. Volume measures the number of shares or contracts traded during the period being analyzed. When volume analysis is combined with candlestick charting, a powerful synergy is formed that provides deeper insight into the mindset of traders. When describing this synergy, I refer to it as the "bark and bite." Price action itself is the bark, and volume confirmation provides the bite, or the conviction behind a price move. Sometimes this is better explained from a statistical standpoint. In conducting a poll, is it better to use a small or a large sample? The larger the sample size is, the more accurate the polling data is likely to be. The same thing holds true with volume. When a price pattern is confirmed by heavy volume, that price pattern has a higher chance of success in terms of its predictability. Price patterns that occur on light or thin volume show a lack of conviction among traders, whereas periods of heavy volume show either strong conviction in a trending market or a struggle for control of price direction at key turning points.

In Chapter 5, in the discussion on trends, I used the analogy of paddling a canoe with or against the current. The price trend is the current, and volume provides a look at the strength of that current and its likelihood of continuing. Just as momentum indicators and moving averages are effective in confirming trends, so too is volume. If a trend is in an uptrend and volume is dropping as the trend continues, the likelihood of a trend slowdown or reversal increases. Increasing volume is not as important in a downtrend, as price often can fall under its own weight simply because of a lack of buying interest. Consistent or increasing volume in a trending market, however, shows that the trend is healthy and there are enough participants to continue to push the price in the direction of the trend. Price rises on increased volume show that more buyers are entering the market (increased demand) and there is not enough supply to meet that demand. Conversely, declining prices on increasing volume show that more sellers are entering the market (increasing supply) and their liquidation is not being met with adequate demand. Several examples of volume and its use with candlesticks will be shown in this chapter, but for anyone wanting to dig deeper into volume analysis, I recommend the book *The Trader's Book of Volume* by Mark Leibovit, which discusses the theory behind volume and the many different types of indicators that can be derived by combining price and volume data.

CONFIRMING CANDLESTICK PATTERNS

Volume plays an important role in candlestick reversal patterns. Whenever a spinning top, doji, hammer, hanging man, or engulfing pattern is formed in a trending market, volume can provide important confirmation regarding the potential success or failure of the pattern. Simply put, the higher the volume when a reversal candle or pattern is formed, the more interaction there is between buyers and sellers. Think of this as sellers increasing their activity in an uptrend because they no longer see present price levels as a good value or as buyers increasing their activity in a downtrend because the decline has been sufficient to make them believe that the security being purchased now has good value. The daily chart of Applied Materials, Inc., in Figure 7-1 shows two reversal patterns confirmed by higher volume.

Applied Materials had been in an uptrend (higher highs and higher lows) before forming the spinning top at point A. As price rose into point A, volume had increased dramatically on the long white candle immediately preceding the spinning top,

FIGURE 7-1

Candlestick Reversals with Volume for Applied Materials, Inc., Daily

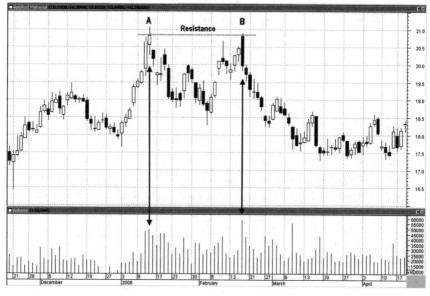

Source: MetaStock

which showed great resolve among the buyers. The very next day, however, the spinning top formed on volume that was even higher than that on the previous long white candle day. This showed that sellers were increasing their activity because all that could be salvaged on such a high-volume day was indecision. The reversal lower off point A also created a short-term top that would act as resistance to any later price advances.

After price chopped lower and reversed higher, it ran smack into the resistance area at point B. Note that the three candles preceding point B were all white, but they were hardly inspiring to the bulls. The opening price of the long black candle at point B formed a rising window relative to the previous day's candle. That window was closed quickly the same day, however, and that gave the action a decidedly bearish tone. What ended up as a bearish engulfing pattern at point B was strongly confirmed by the very heavy volume on that day. This showed exhaustion on the part of buyers as they gapped the price higher at the open but failed to hold the gains. The very heavy volume with the engulfing pattern showed an overwhelming liquidation of positions, which was a strong indication that a lasting top had been made.

Volume also plays an important role in validating candlestick continuation patterns. Since volume is the lifeblood of trends, a sharp increase in volume as an uptrend resumes is a sign of the health of the trend, as an increase in volume shows that new buyers are entering the market to push prices higher. The daily chart of F5 Networks, Inc., in Figure 7-2 demonstrates how volume confirms trend continuation. This is also a chart that includes more than one teachable element, and we will discuss them all.

Before the period shown in the summer and fall of 2001, F5 Networks, Inc., had been in an uptrend, as demonstrated by higher highs and higher lows. As price corrected into the hammer at point A, volume came in at its highest level in over two months

FIGURE 7-2

Candlestick Continuation with Volume for F5 Networks, Inc., Daily

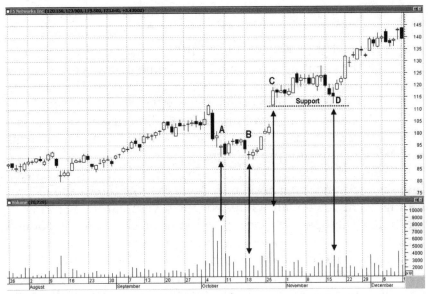

Source: MetaStock

as buyers stepped up to meet the supply of shares being brought to the market by sellers. The increased volume on the hammer formation showed that price was likely to reverse and move higher. Although a reversal did occur, price did not make it very far before once again rolling over and moving lower. At point B, price formed a spinning top just below the hammer formed at point A. The important point here is that as price declined into point B, volume actually *declined* relative to the low made at point A, which showed a lack of selling pressure coming into a support area (the low made at point A). When volume decreases as it approaches support, it is a sign that sellers are not bringing enough supply onto the market to sustain the move lower. This is a bullish indication that selling pressure is waning and that buyers are in a good position to resume the uptrend.

Volume increased after the low at point B, which demonstrated that buyers were reentering the market and pushing prices higher. The rising window formed at point C was accompanied by the heaviest volume in months. A rising window on heavy volume should result in a stronger support area than that provided by a rising window on lower volume. Note that the candle also formed an opening marubozu, which was a good indication that demand was very strong as price opened at its low for the day and never looked back. After a consolidation and pullback period that lasted for three weeks (point D), the uptrend resumed. The high volume on the window opening at point C was an important clue that support was likely to hold at point D.

Volume can confirm or refute candlestick patterns in any time frame. Candlestick/volume reversal patterns formed on weekly charts usually forewarn of larger-impact turning points. The weekly chart of iShares Cohen & Steers Realty ETF in Figure 7-3 shows how candlesticks and volume can work together to provide stronger signals.

The ETF was in a strong uptrend for the period beginning in January 2006. As price advanced, volume was not spectacular but was rather consistent. As price moved sharply higher into its February 2007 top, volume steadily increased, which is healthy for a trend, but it was also a change in character as a normally consistent, unspectacular volume pattern gave way to a pattern

FIGURE 7-3

Weekly Volume Confirming a Reversal for iShares Cohen &
Steers Realty ETF, Weekly

Source: MetaStock

of increasing volume. Remember, a change in volume characteristics is something to look for when one is analyzing volume. A
change in the volume pattern shows a change in trader sentiment.
As price formed the shooting star at point A, volume came in at its
highest level in over a year; that was a dead giveaway that trader
sentiment was changing. The shooting star was formed as buyers
tried to push price out to a new high but failed to hold early gains.
The heavy volume underscored that sentiment because it showed
that a new supply of shares was being brought into the market
by those who wanted to liquidate their positions and take profits.
The next week at point B, a hanging man (very close to being classified as a doji) formed, which showed trader indecision after the
previous week's shooting star failure at a new high. The volume
at point B declined slightly from point A, but remember that each
of these bars was formed over five trading days (one week each),

which was a testament to the struggle that was going on for control of the market. The reversal candle at point B was followed the next week by a black candle, which was a signal that sellers were gaining control.

NONCONFIRMATION OF CANDLESTICK PATTERNS

So far we have examined situations in which volume confirms candlestick lines or patterns. What about times when volume does not show a great deal of conviction among traders? Even in times like these, including volume in your analysis can keep you out of bad or questionable trades. The daily chart of Johnson & Johnson in Figure 7-4 shows a bullish candlestick pattern that was not confirmed by volume.

FIGURE 7-4

Volume Nonconfirmation at Resistance for Johnson & Johnson, Daily

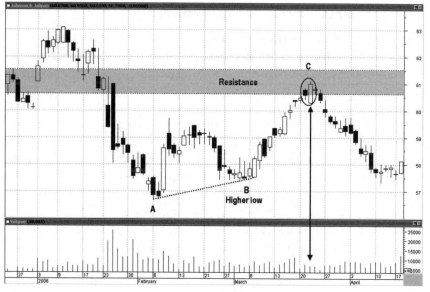

Source: MetaStock

Coming into the low at point A, Johnson & Johnson had been in a downtrend for almost a year. After price bottomed at point A, it rebounded before reversing lower and testing the previous low at point B. The next advance started, which gave indications that a new uptrend was beginning, although the lack of volume after point B cast doubt on the ability of the advance to be sustained. As price continued higher, it came in contact with a prior resistance band consisting of older highs and lows at around $61 (the shaded area). A black spinning top formed into resistance at point C, which showed indecision. This by itself was a warning sign that resistance in this area might be formidable. However, the very next day, a long white candle formed that might have been a green light to some to get long and expect another push higher. Remember that any continuation or bullish patterns that form into resistance are to be treated as suspect. Also note that there was no meaningful increase in volume on the long white candle. A lack of conviction among buyers (low volume) on a candle that formed right at resistance should have been enough to give pause to an astute trader. Sure enough, price reversed lower and moved down below $58 over the next three weeks.

COUNTERTREND BEHAVIOR

The proper interpretation of volume requires an understanding of the trend. Although an increase in volume paired with reversal candles shows high-probability turning points, there are also times when low volume can demonstrate that countertrend buying or selling pressure is running out of steam and that a continuation of the prevailing trend is likely. Volume behavior like this is actually very healthy for the trend in force as it allows traders to take profits along the way. The lower volume signifies that the selling pressure (in an uptrend) or buying pressure (in a downtrend) is not due to a change in sentiment but merely to traders exiting the market in an orderly manner. It is when the volume pattern changes (e.g., an increase in volume as a countertrend move develops) that a trader must be alert for a possible change in trend.

The daily chart of TXN (Texas Instruments Inc.) in Figure 7-5 shows a typical volume pattern for countertrend price moves.

FIGURE 7-5

Countertrend Volume for Texas Instruments Inc., Daily

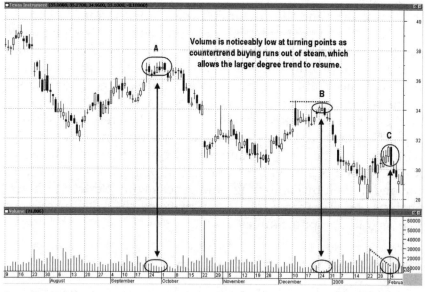

Source: MetaStock

Texas Instruments had topped and begun a downtrend in summer 2007. After price declined and formed a short-term low in August, price rebounded higher into point A, where it formed a number of warning candles (long upper shadows and spinning tops). Note that volume was extremely light during that period compared with its recent past as price pushed into the high at A. The drop in volume showed that the countertrend push higher was not likely to continue. Price managed to chop sideways for another week and a half before the downtrend resumed in earnest.

After the decline off point A, price made another low and rebounded higher into point B. Once again, notice the long upper shadow on very light volume. There was also another piece of evidence in place at point B that increased the likelihood of a reversal lower. Notice that the high at point B ran into resistance that was formed at the high of the black candle on December 11, 2007 (connected by the dotted line). The long upper shadow, light volume, and resistance in place all increased the odds of a price reversal lower. The bearish engulfing pattern the day after the long upper shadow was formed was an indication that the countertrend move was over and the downtrend was ready to resume.

After the high at point B, price declined until two long white candles were formed at the $28 level in January 2008. An interesting development, however, was the decrease in volume as price advanced after the two white candles. Note how volume decreased into the high at point C, where a long black candle signified that the brief recovery was over as sellers resumed control.

This example shows the use of the synergy among candlestick patterns, volume analysis, and support and resistance levels to identify situations in which seemingly strong candlestick patterns can and do fail. By combining candlesticks with Western technical analysis, a trader can develop a multifaceted checklist to accept or bypass trading opportunities.

CANDLEVOLUME CHARTS

A *candlevolume chart* is a chart that combines price and volume in a single plot for purposes of analysis. Candlevolume is based on the equivolume charting methodology developed by Richard Arms, Jr. The only difference is that instead of plotting the hollow boxes used in equivolume charts, the price plot consists of candlesticks whose width is determined by the level of volume for the day. Greg Morris was the first to write about this charting methodology in his article titled "East Meets West: CandlePower Charting" in the December 1990 issue of *Stocks & Commodities* magazine. The name has been changed from CandlePower to candlevolume charting, but the methodology is the same.

Since candlestick charting is superior to the standard bar chart in terms of providing information about the mindset of traders, imagine how much more information a candle can yield when its width is dictated by the level of volume. When one is looking at a candlevolume plot, the width of the candles is set by a normalized volume level of the candles that are displayed. In other words, as the date range on the chart shifts forward and backward, the normalized level of volume can change, and this can affect the width of the candlesticks, depending on how many are displayed, but they will still remain proportionate in relation to one another.

Candlevolume and Trends

The two-dimensional plot of candlevolume charts makes it easier to discern whether a trend is in good health. Remember, consistent or expanding volume is good for the health of a trend. Candlevolume charts provide an easy way to examine the combination of volume and price movement. The daily chart of the PowerShares QQQ Trust ETF in Figure 7-6 shows how consistent width among candlesticks demonstrates consistent volume in a trending market.

Candlevolume charts also lend themselves well to helping traders identify when a trend reversal is likely. The daily chart of Starbucks Corporation in Figure 7-7 shows a great example of price

FIGURE 7-6

Consistent Trend Candlevolume for PowerShares QQQ Trust ETF, Daily

Source: MetaStock

FIGURE 7-7

Slowing Trend Volume Candlevolume for Starbucks
Corporation, Daily

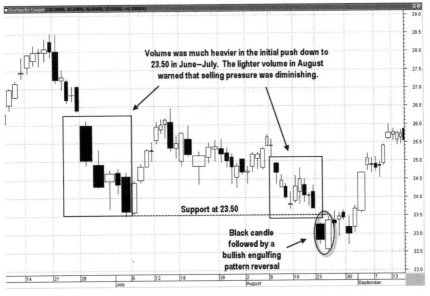

falling into support on lower volume, which increased the odds for
a price reversal higher.

After price topped in June 2010 (left side of the chart) at 28.50,
selling pressure intensified quickly, which pushed price down to
23.50, a loss of 17.5 percent in two weeks. Price bounced higher
before chopping lower and reaching the same price level (23.50) in
August. Notice the width of the candles in the two squares on the
chart. The first square showed very heavy selling pressure as the
candle widths were very wide in relation to the other candles on
the chart. The second square shows much lighter selling pressure
as price approached the support area of 23.50. On August 24, price
breached the 23.50 support line on the heaviest volume since the
initial sell-off in June. The black candle that broke support could
not be considered a long black candle, but the break of support was
noteworthy just the same. It turned out to be the final, exhaustive

push lower for sellers as a bullish engulfing candle that formed the next day showed the resolve of buyers.

Candlevolume and Reversal Patterns

The daily chart of Cisco Systems in Figure 7-8 shows how candle-volume charts can make reversal candles stand out. Cisco had been in a downtrend since November 2007 (not shown). As price declined into a February 7, 2008, low, the candles were getting slightly wider, which signified that volume was increasing. On February 7, price gapped lower before rebounding and forming a bullish piercing line. What really stands out about that particular candle is its width, which demonstrated very strong participation among traders. A white candle of that width in relation to the other candles shows that buyers won the day without question, which

FIGURE 7-8

Candlevolume Chart with Bullish Piercing Line for Cisco Systems, Daily

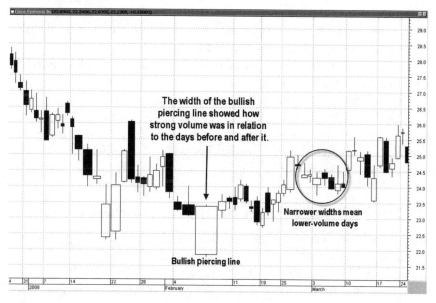

Source: MetaStock

FIGURE 7-9

Candlevolume Chart with Bullish Piercing Line in Longer-
Term View for Cisco Systems, Daily

Source: MetaStock

set a new tone for price direction. This marked the beginning of a
rally phase in which price chopped higher for four months.

Remember that the width of the boxes changes relative to the
other candles shown in the chart. The daily chart of Cisco Systems
has been changed to include more data to illustrate that point in
Figure 7-9. Note how the bullish piercing line candle is narrower
than it was in the preceding example; however, it still stands out
among the surrounding candles because of the heavier volume
posted on that day.

Candlevolume and Support and Resistance

Candlevolume charts also can be used to show high-volume
breaches of support and resistance levels. If support is broken
by a long black candle or if resistance is broken by a long white
candle, it is a noteworthy event. When volume is combined with
the candle plot, however, it can be an eye-opening experience. The

daily chart of Qualcomm Inc. in Figure 7-10 shows how using candlevolume charts can enhance the effect of a break of support.

Price rallied into the August 2008 high on the left side of the
chart before beginning a modest decline. In early September, price
found support at the 45 level and chopped sideways for most of
the month. On September 29, price decisively broke down through
support at 45 with a wide, long black candle. Events like this show
the effectiveness of candlevolume charts as the candle that broke
support stood out from the other candles that surrounded it. Candlevolume charts make it easier to find important reversal and continuation patterns.

The major drawback to using candlevolume charts is that the
width of the candles can result in fewer candlesticks being displayed on the chart. This gives less information to the trader, such
as potential support and resistance areas that may be cut off. The
differing widths of the candles also distort the time axis, which is

FIGURE 7-10

Candlevolume Chart with Break of Support for Qualcomm
Inc., Daily

Source: MetaStock

used in cycle analysis. The distorted time scale also hinders the drawing of effective trendlines. Candlevolume charts do have their place if a trader chooses to use them. Just make sure to check a longer-term view to show support and resistance areas that may be more visible on a standard candlestick chart.

THINKING OUTSIDE THE BOX

The examples given above are textbook examples of "proper" volume behavior such as increasing on breakouts or breakdowns and increasing or being steady during market trends. Since the March 2009 low, however, the use of volume in broad market analysis has been frustrating to many as volume has not always confirmed price moves higher even though the overall market uptrend lasted for over two years. Also, since the March 2009 low, volume patterns have changed in selected stocks or ETFs along with sharp increases in volatility. In my opinion, there are two reasons for this. The reason for higher volatility is high-frequency trading in which large blocks of shares are traded purely to scalp small profits by capitalizing on minuscule pricing inefficiencies; this can cause higher volume totals and volatile price movement with little correlation to true buying and selling by real traders. High frequency trading is driven by automated algorithms that continually monitor stocks and place buy and sell orders throughout the day on the basis of predetermined conditions for trade entry and exit. A probable reason for the broad market uptrend on lower volume since the 2008 market meltdown is that the average investor for the most part has steered clear of stocks. This in effect unmasks the activity of the banks and other large players that have been able to push the market indexes higher on low-volume days. In many cases gains are made in the premarket futures with little price movement during the actual trading day. This is possible because it takes fewer dollars to drive the futures market than it does to buy shares during the regular open trading session.

In spite of these recent characteristics that have compromised the reliability of volume, there are more creative ways in which volume can be used. This is where thinking outside the box can serve a trader well. In the following examples I will share an indicator that I created that is driven off the cumulative volume of the top 10 stocks in Market Vectors Gold Miners ETF. The top 10 stocks in this ETF account for over 70 percent of its holdings. Although using the actual volume of more liquid ETFs is valid, one must remember that ETFs themselves are derivatives in that they derive their value from the stocks included in their calculation. In other words, if it were not for the stocks within an ETF, that ETF would have no value. This creates a situation, however, that we can use to our advantage. If we analyze the volume of the actual components of an ETF, a clearer picture can be obtained of whether the ETF trend is likely to continue or if a change in price direction is due. This indicator is not exclusive to Market Vectors Gold Miners ETF but can be constructed by using any ETF or index.

I call this indicator the Volume Percentage Indicator (VPI). The psychology behind the indicator is that when the VPI reaches a value of 70 percent or above, it shows that volume flows are reaching an extreme positive level off of which sellers tend to emerge, which can cause price to reverse lower. When the VPI reaches a value of 30 percent or below, it shows that volume flows are reaching an extreme negative level off of which value buyers tend to emerge or short sellers begin to cover their positions, which cause price to rise. These events may not lead to changes in the direction of the overall trend, but they regularly provide great opportunities for short-term trading. The construction of the VPI is based on the same concept used for the On Balance Volume Indicator in that when the security closes higher on the day, all of its volume is seen as positive. When the security closes lower on the day, all of its volume is seen as negative. The difference here is that I do that for each of the top 10 holdings in Market Vectors Gold Miners ETF and then aggregate the positive and negative volumes to create a percentage of positive volume among the top 10 Market Vectors Gold Miners ETF stocks.

For example, at the time of this writing, one of the top 10 holdings of Market Vectors Gold Miners ETF is Barrick Gold Corporation. If Barrick closed higher on the day, all of Barrick's volume goes into the positive column. Another top 10 stock in Market Vectors Gold Miners ETF is Newmont Mining Corporation. If on the same day Newmont closed lower, all of Newmont's volume would be added to the negative column. This is done for each stock, and the subsequent volume is added to either the positive or the negative column. If the stock closed unchanged, no volume would be added to either column. To compute the VPI, divide the aggregate positive volume by the total volume (positive plus negative) for the day of the 10 stocks and multiply by 100. In its raw form, the indicator is unusable, as shown in Figure 7-11.

Note how the indicator fluctuates widely between 0 and 100, with 100 percent days meaning that every one of the stocks that had a price change from the previous day closed higher, which resulted in all of the day's volume being positive; 0 percent days mean that all of the stocks that had a price change from the previous day closed lower, resulting in all of the day's volume being negative. So how do we get the indicator into a usable form? This is accomplished by smoothing the indicator with a moving average of its values. In this case, we will use a 10-day simple moving average. Notice how the indicator is much easier to interpret in Figure 7-12.

FIGURE 7-11

Raw VPI

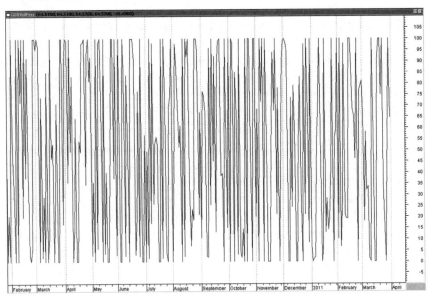

Source: MetaStock

FIGURE 7-12

Smoothed VPI

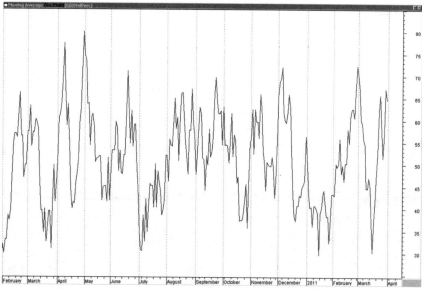

Source: MetaStock

Now that the indicator is in a usable form, let's plot it below the price plot of Market Vectors Gold Miners ETF to see what we have. I have added horizontal lines at the 70 and 30 levels. Notice in Figure 7-13 that when the VPI peaks at or above 70, price *tends* to reverse lower, and that whenever the VPI makes a low at or below 30, price *tends* to reverse higher. Each of these instances is marked with a vertical dashed line. Also notice that some reversals were sharp and some were not much of a reversal at all. No indicator is perfect. These VPI reversals show when a short-term change in price direction is likely, but not necessarily a change in the overall trend.

By pairing the VPI with candlesticks, we can get a two-dimensional look at the psychology of traders by using both price data (candlesticks) and volume (VPI). Figure 7-14 shows the synergy created by combining candlesticks and the VPI. The points of interest are labeled A through F.

At point A, price made its closing high as the VPI peaked over 70 (see the two-sided arrow). The VPI move above 70 percent

FIGURE 7-13

Smoothed VPI with Market Vectors Gold Miners ETF, Daily

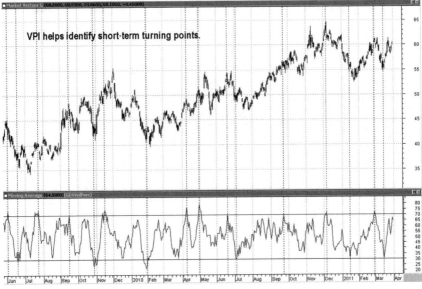

Source: MetaStock

showed that trader psychology was ready to shift as the positive sentiment shown by the positive volume flows was reaching extreme levels. This gave the bearish engulfing pattern that formed the very next day much more weight as a valid reversal signal that a change in price direction was due. Market Vectors Gold Miners ETF declined into point B, where the VPI fell briefly below 30 percent. Should a trader looking for a bounce here have bought blindly just because the VPI was below 30 percent? Of course not. Take a look at the candlesticks that were formed the two days after point B. There was nothing there that showed that a reversal higher was due as a weak spinning top was followed by a long black candle. There was no reason to take a long trade there. Price continued lower into point C, but note the positive divergence shown in the VPI as price made a lower low but the VPI made a higher low.

This was an indication that positive volume flows were coming back into the top 10 components of Market Vectors Gold Miners

FIGURE 7-14

Trading Using the VPI for Market Vectors Gold Miners ETF, Daily

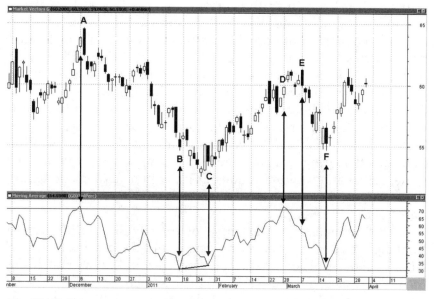

ETF. There was also flat resistance at the 55 price level formed by the falling window just after point B. Market Vectors could have been purchased as price broke up through 55 with a white candle as the VPI continued to trend higher, showing that volume flows were supportive. As price moved higher into point D, the VPI also made a peak over 70. This was a difficult environment to trade for a few days, however, as the price action became gapped and choppy. This was an indication that buyers and sellers were battling for control of the short-term price direction. The candles formed between points D and E were hardly compelling enough to show that a reversal lower was developing, but by the time price rallied up to point E, the handwriting was on the wall.

Notice how as price moved higher from point D, the VPI already was trending lower, showing that volume flows were not supporting higher prices. This situation gave the bearish engulfing pattern at point E much more weight as a valid reversal signal that had to be heeded. Price moved lower once again to point F, where the VPI touched the 30 percent level. After the bearish black candle at point F, a doji formed the very next day, followed by a rising window. Although the candle that formed the rising window also formed a spinning top, the fact that buyers were able to hold prices higher on the day along with the now rising VPI showed that taking a long-side trade would be worth the risk as the rising window was accompanied by positive volume flows.

Can the reliability of the volume of the stocks used in the calculation of the VPI fall victim to current market issues such as high-frequency trading? Of course it can, but this demonstration indicates that even during these interesting times in which we trade, aggregating volume among ETF components and combining them with candlesticks can help you look at ETF trading in a whole new light.

This is merely one example of how with a little creative thinking a trader can gain extra insight into the price behavior of ETFs or indexes. I am always playing with indicators and using their root concepts to attempt to create something new. As your understanding of both price- and volume-based indicators evolves, you may find yourself creating an indicator that can enhance your trading results. Never be afraid to explore and try new things.

SUMMARY

Volume is a very important yet often overlooked tool in market analysis. Although candlestick lines and patterns give much more information to a trader than a standard bar chart does, adding volume shows the strength or conviction behind those patterns. Volume can alert a trader to whether a reversal or continuation pattern is likely to succeed or fail as volume analysis gives a deeper look into the mindset or mood of market participants. Candle-volume charts combine volume with candlesticks to give an inclusive picture in one plot, which eliminates the need to plot volume in a separate window. Although candlevolume charts can be convenient, there are drawbacks, such as less information being displayed on the chart during high-volume periods (as a result of increased candle widths) and a distortion of the time axis, which can hinder cyclical analysis and the drawing of accurate trendlines. Although volume has its place historically in market analysis, its value has become distorted over the last couple of years by high-frequency trading as well as market manipulation via the futures market. By thinking outside the box and coming up with new ideas, you can gain deeper insights and your trading results can be enhanced. Never be afraid to explore new possibilities with volume-based indicators.

CHAPTER 8

Accumulating Evidence and Assembling the Pieces

Have you ever had one of those "duh" moments when you smacked yourself in the head because a mistake you made could have been avoided? I had my share of those enlightening moments in my early trading days. Through trial and error, I began to add pieces to a trading puzzle that allowed me to see the markets more clearly. This chapter will help you assemble the pieces you have been given to get an accurate picture of market conditions that will enable you to make informed trading decisions.

The first seven chapters examined how candlesticks are constructed, candlestick reversal patterns, candlestick continuation patterns, trends, support and resistance, momentum indicators, and different ways to use and interpret volume. Understanding these topics and putting them together will allow you to develop a solid foundation for trading success. As each tool has been added to our analysis arsenal, I have been using the term *weight of the evidence* to describe how technical analysis can be used to enhance a trader's odds for success. Although candlesticks on their own are an effective method for analyzing the mindset of market participants, adding tools that can support the messages given by candlestick lines and patterns will make it clearer which patterns should yield winning trades and which patterns are best avoided.

Putting all the pieces together gives trading ideas a level of synergy that the individual pieces cannot achieve on their own.

Think of a trader in the same light as a carpenter building a house. Each has a wide array of tools at his or her disposal. Would the carpenter try to build a house with just a hammer? Wouldn't using a saw, a tape measure, a level, and so on, yield a better end product? Then why on earth do new traders use just one indicator? This chapter will take a look at three different trading scenarios and discuss how best to trade them. By learning to recognize the characteristics of market situations as they develop, you will have the tools at your disposal to succeed in any market environment.

Any discussion about trading would not be complete without mentioning risk. A trader can mitigate risk by trading in the direction of the market trend and also by using stop orders. Stop orders are very important in that they are a trader's exit point for trades that no longer meet the criteria for taking them. For example, if a trader buys a position that is based on an upside reversal and price breaks below the extreme of the reversal candle or pattern, an upside reversal no longer exists. A stop order would be executed automatically to close the position. A successful trader has to be disciplined. This means sticking to his or her trading rules regardless of emotion. The worst thing a trader can do is to rationalize holding on to a position when the reason for taking that position no longer exists. Continuing to hold that position turns what was meant to be a short-term trade into a longer, more painful "buy and hope" trade. Traders who have a plan and stick to it are doing their part to mitigate risk by not leaving their trading accounts open to large losses.

When you are trading by using price patterns and momentum, always trade what you see, not what you *want* to see or what you *think* you should see. Again, if the reason for taking the trade no longer exists, get out! You can spend much time trying to convince yourself that you are right and the market is wrong. The market is never wrong. The battlefield of trading is littered with the careers of those who thought they were right and the market eventually would see things their way. If you insist on fighting the market and rationalizing why you are doing that, donate your trading account to charity because you will end up losing it anyway. That doesn't mean that countertrend situations cannot be traded successfully, but if you are new to the trading game, I suggest starting out with more conservative trades that are in agreement with the inter- mediate- or longer-term trend. This will allow you to commit pieces of your capital to accumulating positions as the trend pauses, using the existing energy or flow of the market in your favor.

I also strongly suggest that as you view the charts in this chapter, you use something to cover up the charts past the point being discussed in each example. For example, if I am discussing point A, cover up the remainder of the chart to the right of that point. The reason for doing this is that as trading opportunities unfold in the real world, there are no data to the right to verify whether a trade will be successful. Stepping through the examples in this way will give you a better feel for what you will see as opportunities present themselves.

TRADING WITH THE TREND

Trading with the trend or adding positions off countertrend pullbacks is a lower-risk method for making profits. As was dis- cussed in Chapter 5, when a trend is in force, the overall energy is flowing in one direction much like the current in a river. Using this energy allows small traders to hitch a ride with the big boys and profit from the current that is carrying prices higher or lower. In utilizing this methodology, it is best to analyze the volume pattern to make sure volume does not increase during countertrend moves or pullbacks against the trend. Also include a shorter-term momentum indicator that reaches overbought and oversold levels more easily than longer-term (smoother) momentum indicators.

Using this methodology allows a trader to add more positions as the trend develops and matures. This means that early in the trend, only a percentage of tradable capital should be invested in the position, not the whole enchilada. From there, positions are added on subsequent pullbacks as the trend matures. One of the nice features of this methodology is that it generally allows for lower-risk trades because the stops are placed close to the buy point at the swing lows and can be moved up along the way below subsequent swing lows for all the positions taken during the trend. A weight of the evidence methodology will be used for each trade, with the candlestick pattern, momentum indicator, and volume all being given consideration to determine that a valid buy point has been reached.

The daily chart of Applied Materials, Inc. in Figure 8-1 shows an example of adding positions in a trending market. The price plot is overlaid with a 40-day simple moving average (SMA) to help assess the trend. Below the price plot is a five-period slow stochastic (5, 3, 3) and a plot of volume. The shorter setting of the slow stochastic (five periods) will allow it to reach overbought and oversold levels in trending markets more easily, which suits our purpose here. As in Chapter 6, all references to the stochastic use the %K (solid) line.

The uptrend was established in the lower left section of the chart as price climbed above the 40-day SMA just before the moving average turned higher. Once the uptrend had begun (higher price highs and lows with a rising moving average), each time the stochastic oscillator reached the oversold zone (below 20), a two-sided

FIGURE 8-1

Trading with the Trend for Applied Materials, Inc., Daily

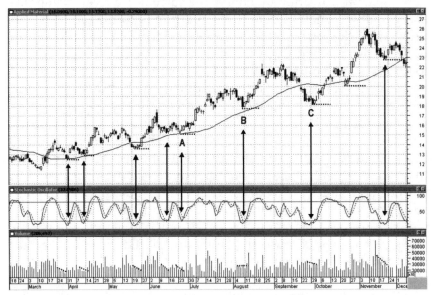

Source: MetaStock

arrow was drawn between price and the stochastic. The volume plot (shown in the bottom pane) has dotted lines drawn across the tops of the volume bars as the stochastic reached oversold territory. Volume is a very important piece of the puzzle as it was level or declined heading into each low. The fact that volume did not intensify during pullbacks was a positive sign for the uptrend and increased the odds that the trend would continue.

Finally, notice the horizontal dotted lines drawn below each pullback in the price plot, which signify where stops should be placed for each trade. The theory here is that each time price pulls back and the trend resumes, a new position should be purchased and the stops for *all* positions accumulated during the uptrend should be moved up to just below the most recent swing low. This allows profits to be locked in on earlier positions if the trend reverses and also provides a close stop for the most recent purchase. Granted, this is a chart that was selected after the fact, and so finding a nice long uptrend and presenting it are easy. The true test comes in real time when the chart stops at the most recent candle and there is nothing to give you an idea of what may come next except the trend and your trusted indicators. I will zoom in and step you through three trades at points A, B, and C on the chart and the thought process behind them.

Figure 8-2 is a zoomed-in version of Figure 8-1 with an emphasis on the three trade points A, B, and C. At each point there are two lines drawn. The horizontal solid line is resistance to be used as a buy trigger, and the horizontal dotted line is the level below which to place a price stop. The resistance lines are drawn above the tops of the highest point of the most recent black candle(s) as price headed into the low. Buys were triggered when the following occurred:

- The stochastic touched oversold territory (20 or lower).
- The price action formed a candlestick reversal pattern.
- Price *closed* over resistance on an increase in volume that showed that the trend was ready to resume.

There are actually two buy points at point A as a double bottom formed at support just above the 40-day SMA. The first buy point formed a spinning top as the stochastic touched the 20

F I G U R E   8 - 2

Trading with the Trend (Zoomed In) for Applied Materials, Inc., Daily

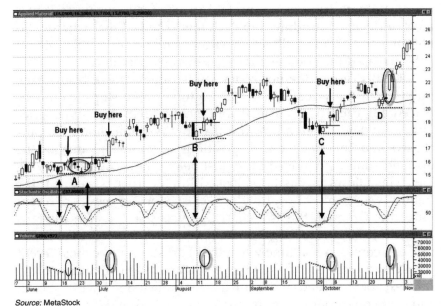

level on declining volume. Remember, the declining volume shows weak selling pressure, which signals that the uptrend is likely to resume once profit takers have finished liquidating their positions. The extreme of the upper shadow of the spinning top was used as resistance. Price declined into the low before moving higher for three straight sessions. The third candle was a white candle that broke resistance and had a noticeable increase in volume, showing that buyers were returning to the market. A protective price stop should have been placed just below the June 13 swing low. If price moved below that low price, the position should have been exited. The subsequent move higher was short-lived, however, as price once again rolled lower and touched the 40-day SMA to test support.

Note again that volume declined heading into the low and the stochastic once again touched the 20 level. As price pulled back, it formed two spinning tops and an inverted hammer (circled). Price never dipped below the stop price level, however, and so the position taken earlier was still intact. In this case the resistance line was drawn at the swing high (the black candle immediately after the previous buy). Price chopped around for seven days before finally exploding higher with a long white candle on a large increase in volume (circled below). This was a definite signal that buyers were ready once again to bid Applied Materials, Inc., shares higher. Since the buy points were very close, it was okay to use the same price stop that was used on the first purchase.

At point B another buying opportunity developed. Price once again pulled back as the stochastic dipped below the 20 level. In this case volume remained flat, which showed no alarming increase in the conviction of sellers during the decline. Again, this was healthy behavior for the uptrend. Resistance is drawn from the top of the long black candle that formed at point B. Price pushed higher for three straight days before breaking up through resistance on a long white candle with another jump in volume. The August 8 low point at B now is used as a price stop, and the stops for *all* positions should have been moved up to just below the point B low. Moving the stops higher means that you are virtually guaranteeing yourself a profit as the stop is now in the $18 area for positions that were purchased earlier at around $15.

Point C is an interesting situation in that price broke down through its 40-day SMA yet there still was a pattern of higher highs and higher lows, which meant that the uptrend was intact. Any time a moving average is breached this seriously, it is cause for concern, but using our definition of an uptrend, there was still something to work with. Besides, since this pullback took price back near the latest stop level (just below point B), this could be viewed as a lower-risk opportunity to enter the trend if it resumed. As price moved lower into point C, notice two things. First, volume was declining as price moved lower, which was a sign that sellers lacked the conviction necessary to drive price sharply lower. Second, the stochastic was showing a positive divergence as price made a lower low but the stochastic made a higher low.

This was a huge warning sign that price was likely to reverse higher. Since price was still technically in an uptrend, this was a lower-risk buying opportunity. A resistance line was drawn off the top of the black candle that formed as price headed into the low. It is important to remember that in this example buys are not executed unless price *closes* over resistance. This ensures that buying pressure was enough to keep price over resistance for the day, thus avoiding the intraday head fake that happens when price pops up through resistance before reversing and closing lower. Waiting to make sure the close was above resistance would have saved some angst at point C as the second day after the low, price broke up through resistance intraday but closed below as it formed an inverted hammer. Also notice that volume was very low, which was a signal that buyers were not yet ready to resume the uptrend.

The next day, October 3, a long hammer was formed, closing well above the resistance line on heavier volume (circled below). The hammer on October 3 was a definite buy signal as sellers tried to take the price lower after a rising window on the open. Buyers fought back, which brought the closing price back up very close to the gap higher open and caused price to close well above resistance. The stop should have been raised for *all* positions to just below the September 29 low at point C. From that point forward, simply raising the stops to just below the most recent swing lows as they developed would have been a nice way to trail price higher with the protective stop ready to lock in profits if the trend reversed.

On Figure 8-2 I have added point D, which was a good trading opportunity even though the stochastic did not reach oversold territory (below 20). For that reason it was not included in the series, as it did not have all the weight of the evidence indicators in its favor. This is, however, a great example of Applied Materials finding support at its 40-day SMA, which was a sign that the uptrend was healthy. Also notice the increase in volume on the rising window formed immediately after the spinning top that was developed right on top of the 40-day SMA (both circled). This means that a trade could have been taken there with a reasonable expectation of success as a large white candle gapped higher on strong volume off support. Whether the trade was taken or not, the stops for all positions acquired during the trend should have been moved up to just below the swing low at point D.

TRADING SWING POINTS

Although trading with the trend is a great way to build profits patiently in the direction of the trend, trading swing points is another way to lock in quick profits as markets change direction. This method is slightly more risky simply because a trader now is trying to trade shorter-term tops and bottoms, but there is no reason a disciplined trader following a sound set of rules should not be successful. The main difference between trading with the trend and trading swings is that in trading swings, trades are taken in both directions regardless of the trend. Trading against the trend is tantamount to paddling against the current of the river, but with the tools available (candlesticks, momentum, volume, and stops) more experienced traders have enough pieces of information to be able to make sound trading decisions.

The daily chart of Greenhill & Co. in Figure 8-3 shows an example of swing points that can be exploited for profit. In this example, a 10-day price rate of change is used along with volume. The rate of change indicator will provide insight into the velocity of price movement whether the movement is positive or negative

FIGURE 8-3

Trading Swing Points for Greenhill & Co., Daily

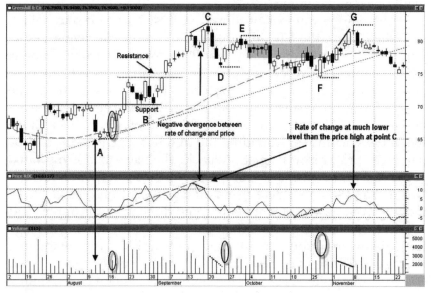

Source: MetaStock

by its proximity to the zero line as well as overbought/oversold levels to give an idea of whether price is in a position where it is likely to reverse direction. It is always important to understand the indicators you select for use; this is akin to a carpenter using the right tool for the job.

Remember that the rate of change indicator can give different overbought and oversold levels, depending on the time period chosen, the security it is being applied to, and the trend. After first examining the behavior of the rate of change before the period shown on the chart, I determined that the best levels to look for reversals are 10 for overbought and −5 for oversold. This example again will use the 40-day SMA (the dashed line on the price plot) as another tool for determining trend and also for defining possible support and resistance levels. Finally, notice the upsloping trendline that is drawn from left to right on the chart (the dotted upsloping line in the price plot). It is always convenient to show after the fact chart examples, and so it is important to realize that as this sequence was unfolding, the trendline did not exist until the swing low at point A was formed. When the initial low on the left side of the chart was connected with the swing low at point A and the line was extended, potential support areas would be evident in the future.

There are a number of things on this chart to discuss. First, note the low on the left side of the chart before the swing low at point A. A bullish engulfing candle formed on strong volume, which demonstrated that the previous downtrend was likely over and that buyers were assuming control of price direction. The 40-day SMA also changed direction shortly thereafter, going from down to up. This type of action should prompt a trader to wait for the initial volatility surrounding the trend change to wane and be patient as price forms its first pullback. The place to look for initial support is in the vicinity of the 40-day SMA. Even though the first two examples shown here use a 40-day SMA, the *concept* of the moving average as an identifier of trend direction and support and resistance is more important than the length of the moving average itself. Remember, you can use whatever length and type of moving average you wish to complement your trading time frame.

As price pulled back into the swing low at point A, a spinning top was formed on the day price touched the moving average.

The spinning top followed a rather ominous-looking black candle on the previous day; that showed that the selling pressure shown by the black candle already was beginning to dissipate. A look at the volume on the day of the black candle, however, showed that there was not much conviction among sellers, which gave even more weight to the spinning top. The next-day price gapped higher which formed a rather weak-looking morning star reversal pattern. As the price moved lower into the morning star reversal, the rate of change indicator descended and managed to touch the oversold level of –5, which was an indication that a change of direction higher was due for price. On the third day after the initial spinning top at point A, a long white candle formed on the heaviest volume in over two weeks (circled). The white candle also used the 40-day SMA as support before launching higher, which showed that a new uptrend was beginning. This was the signal to initiate a long position with a stop placed just below the swing low at point A (the horizontal dotted line).

After the buy at point A, price moved higher with a couple of shorter white candles as price encountered a resistance area around 70 (the solid line), which is where the original pullback into point A originated. Volume increased, which showed the struggle between buyers and sellers at this price level, but on August 20 price broke up through resistance on a long white candle with very heavy volume. This allowed a nice profit for a swing trader. Those looking for a quick profit could exit here, whereas those looking for more substantial profits could move their stop up just below the low of the long white candle on August 23. Moving the stop employs the principle that what was once resistance is now support. If that support were broken, the health of the uptrend would become suspect and moving to the sidelines would be wise.

On August 26 a black candle formed that closed the rising window that had opened on August 23. Again, those looking for a quicker exit could have sold their position here and those looking for more profit could have held with their stop safely below 70. After three straight black candles, a new long white candle was formed, but the rate of change indicator was already above the overbought level of 10. This was an indication that more patience was required as price had to consolidate further before the uptrend resumed. Price pulled back one more time to point B, where the

70 level was providing solid support. Very little consideration was given to shorting at the point B high because of the support level at 70. Even if that support level was broken, the rising 40-day SMA and rising trendline offered new support areas that should have limited downside price movement. The rate of change also exhibited strong trending characteristics off its low that coincided with the low at point A (shown by the dashed line on the rate of change indicator in the middle pane of the chart). As price chopped around at point B, a new resistance level was formed at 74 that was touched three times.

Note that on the final day below that resistance line, volume increased and the long white candle closed right at resistance. The strong close on higher volume was an indication that the resistance level might give way. Price finally broke up through that level on September 4 as the rate of change indicator was well below the overbought level. Even though volume dropped slightly on the breakout day, the action of the previous day (closing at the resistance line on increasing volume) helped the bullish case as any further upside momentum would result in a break of the resistance line. New buyers as well as those still holding from the initial purchase at point A could move their stop level up to just below the resistance now turned support level at 74 (the horizontal thin dotted line above point B).

Price moved higher into point C, which developed into the first legitimate opportunity to scalp some short-side profits in the uptrend. There are two very important things to note about the rate of change indicator as price advanced into point C. First, the ROC was into overbought territory as the high was formed, which provided evidence that a change in price direction might have been due. Second, note how the rate of change indicator ran into resistance at the extended momentum trendline that was drawn off the rate of change low that coincided with point A. The facts that the rate of change indicator was overbought and that it was running into resistance were two compelling pieces of evidence that this trade was worth examining more closely.

Just before point C, a long white candle was formed with heavy volume on September 13, which reinforced the strength of the uptrend. The very next day (September 14), however, a spinning top (almost a doji) formed, which showed trader indecision. This spinning top was noteworthy because it formed just after the long white candle and also because volume did not drop that much from the previous day. The elevated volume total demonstrated that sellers were entering the market to unload their shares and the supply of shares they sold was enough to stop the advance in its tracks. An aggressive trader could have shorted after the spinning top as a black candle formed that took out the low of the spinning top. There is one issue with that, though. Notice how volume dropped on the black candle, which showed that sellers probably lacked the conviction to take the market lower at that point. For those who chose to short anyway, placing a top just above the high of the spinning top would limit risk and make this trade worth a shot.

Two days later (September 17) price moved higher once again, this time on another white candle with heavy volume that was the heaviest since the low at point A. For those who initiated a trade on the September 14 spinning top, their protective buy stop would have taken them out of their short position. Was this another breakout like the two previous breakouts off the lows of point A and point B? One disturbing aspect of this candle is the length of its lower shadow. The longer lower shadow showed that sellers were bringing more shares to the market and for a time were bringing enough supply to force price lower. Buyers eventually prevailed, but it was a struggle. The very next day (September 20) price gapped higher before forming a spinning top that showed more trader indecision. Volume did indeed drop again from the very high level posted on the previous day, but take a look at the rate of change indicator.

Remember how the ROC indicator ran into resistance at the extension of its previous up trendline? It turned lower after that and made a *lower high* while price made a *higher high*. This formed a negative divergence, which was another piece of evidence that tilted the odds of a successful trade in our favor and provided enough evidence that taking a trade on a reversal lower would be a good opportunity. A short trade could have been initiated once the low of the spinning top candle was taken out with a stop placed just above the high of the spinning top candle at point C (the dotted line). Those who initiated long positions off the point A or point B low should have locked in profit here if they hadn't done so already.

A spinning top reversal coupled with the ROC divergence showed that a spirited pullback was possible. The distance between the high at point C down to the 40-day SMA and the trendline (both areas of support) also made this an attractive trade.

As price moved lower into point D, volume declined, which showed a lack of conviction among sellers. The low-volume spinning top on September 23 was an indication that a pop higher in price might be coming. The rate of change indicator had pulled back to the zero line, which is the dividing line between positive and negative momentum. The zero line provides support or resistance in many cases as well. So we had a pullback on declining volume, our momentum indicator sitting on possible support, and a spinning top. This also could have been a signal to lock in profit from the short trade off the high at point C.

Remember, price was still in an overall uptrend, and so it would not have been wise to overstay one's welcome with countertrend positions. If a chance presents itself to lock in a profit on a countertrend trade, one should take it and wait for the next opportunity. On September 24, a long white candle formed on heavy volume (circled), which signaled that this brief pullback was over and that a long position should be taken. The stop should have been placed below the low of the spinning top at point D (the dotted line). Would the uptrend resume? It certainly looked possible, but we always must be vigilant in analyzing the collective actions of traders. One point of reference to consider here is that the resistance area formed overhead at point C was looming just above current levels.

Price rebounded into point E but could get no further as a spinning top formed just as price broke above 80 in the vicinity of the point C high. Another piece of evidence here is that the real bodies of the candles heading into the high at point E were small. Also notice that the rate of change indicator was chopping around the zero line, which showed a relative absence of upside momentum even as price moved higher for a few days heading into point E. Volume was also lackluster as buyers seemed reluctant to push price higher as they had done in the past. A new short trade could have been initiated as the low of the spinning top at point E was taken out. A protective buy stop should have been placed over the high of the spinning top at point E (the dotted line).

Price finally broke lower after point E and declined into point F. Along the way there was one point where a trade could have been considered (the long white candle on October 21), but that candle ran straight into the resistance area caused by the price consolidation after the swing high at point E (the shaded area). The resistance area increased the odds that the trade would not be successful, and so it was wise to wait for a better opportunity. As price declined into the 75 area at point F, there were two previous lows in the weeks before at the same level, which was a clue to look for some sort of support there.

Also note that the rising window that opened back in early September at the 75 level also was providing solid support. The decline into point F featured an inverted hammer that showed that selling interest was waning. Also, the rising up trendline drawn off the price low on the extreme left side of the chart was coming back into play as support. Volume also increased as the inverted hammer formed, which showed increased conviction among buyers as support at 75 held. The rate of change indicator also was beginning to make a series of higher lows, which showed latent momentum strength. Things were shaping up for a great trading opportunity. On October 27, a long white candle formed on very heavy volume (circled). This was a sign that a new push higher was beginning. A new long trade should have been initiated with a protective stop just below the low of the long white candle at point F (the dotted line).

As price pushed higher into point G, volume began to decline conspicuously (solid lines on the price and volume plots). Declining volume as price approached prior resistance (created at point C) was something that should have gotten traders salivating as a great short trading opportunity was likely to present itself. Not only was volume weak, note where the rate of change indicator was in relation to its position at point C on the chart. Recall that at point C the ROC was in overbought territory (over 10), whereas heading into point G it was well below that level, another red flag.

As price reached the same level as the point C high, a doji formed on November 8, which was an indication that price would likely not be able to break through resistance. This would have been a great opportunity for traders holding long positions off the point F low to lock in profits. Our weight of the evidence methodology has a doji backed up by declining volume and weak upward price momentum right at resistance, which presented a compelling short trading opportunity. The very next day a long black candle formed with a slight increase in volume, which when grouped with the other evidence provided enough information to initiate a short trade. A protective stop should have been placed above the doji high at point G (the dotted line). Following the point G high, the price broke down through the 40-day SMA as well as the upsloping trend line. The break of two support areas showed that the uptrend was likely over.

This swing trading example may have seemed a bit drawn out and wordy, but it is important for you to learn to study trading opportunities as they present themselves and look at possible trades from all angles, such as candlestick patterns, support and resistance, momentum, and volume. It is through this repetition that you will develop your trading skill and learn to recognize trades that have a high potential for success.

TRADING WEEKLY BREAKOUTS

Some of the most profitable trades occur on weekly range breakouts. Waiting for these patterns to develop and resolve themselves in one direction or the other requires much patience, but the subsequent price moves can be quite rewarding. As opposed to trading in the intraday and daily time frames, executing trades in the weekly time frame requires a much lower investment of time as each candle represents the cumulative action of five trading days. Remember, when one is trading off weekly charts, it is wise to wait until Friday to get an accurate picture of the collective trading action for the week that forms the candlestick pattern. Jumping too soon on a weekly candle can lead to bad trades and unnecessary losses. Think of patience in the weekly time frame as a daily equity trader placing a trade at 1 p.m. on the basis of a candlestick pattern when there are still three hours to go in the trading day. These last few hours (or days in the weekly time frame) can mean the difference between a doji and an engulfing pattern being formed. The relationship between the opening and closing prices is what makes candlesticks unique, and so waiting as close to the closing price as possible is prudent.

The weekly chart of CBOT (Chicago Board of Trade) continuous contract soybeans in Figure 8-4 shows how the candlesticks, the momentum indicator [in this case a 14-period relative strength index (RSI)], and volume all combined to give a clear signal for the proper time to place a trade. The two horizontal dashed lines drawn across the chart delineate the price range formed by price points A through E. Price ranges are common occurrences after sharp declines as volatility reverts to its mean.

In June–July 2005, soybeans formed a top on the left side of the chart at the 750 level. After the top, prices declined into low point A. About halfway through the move lower in August, a falling window formed between 640 and 642, which as you have learned should provide resistance to subsequent price advances. As price came into its point A low in December 2005, it actually undercut the prior low made in October. As price made a lower

FIGURE 8-4

Weekly Breakout Trade for CBOT Soybeans Continuous Contract, Weekly

Source: MetaStock

low, however, the RSI made a higher low, which was a positive divergence that is shown by the solid lines. The divergence with the long white candle and the increase in volume on the white candle at point A (circled) showed that the decline off the summer 2005 high was probably over.

Price moved higher into point B, where a long white candle on good volume was followed by a hanging man and another black candle. Volume waned when the hanging man was formed but increased markedly with the black candle. The message given by the market in this case was that buyers tried to rally the price higher but failed miserably as the jump in volume (circled below) indicated. The falling window formed in August also provided resistance that made the bearish combination of candles at point B that much stronger, making price likely to reverse lower.

Now that the low at point A and the high at point B have been established, we can see the range beginning to take shape. Since we now have the point A low in place, the decline off the high at point B should be expected to find support in that area. As price declined into point C, notice that the RSI was bottoming in the same place as it did in point A, whereas price made a slightly higher low but was still in the vicinity of the point A low. Volume was consistent as the bullish harami and spinning top (both in the same candle) formed at point C. The long white candle that formed as price reversed higher off the point C low was on a sharp increase in volume, which indicated that the point C low was in place.

As price advanced higher into point D, the RSI was finding resistance at the same level it achieved as price made its point B high (the dotted line on the RSI plot). This development is a valuable tool that can be used to see if momentum confirms a price breakout. At the point D high, notice that a doji and a spinning top were formed as price encountered dual resistance formed by the falling window and the point B high. Volume also increased from the doji to the spinning top, which showed once again that buyers probably were not going to be able to cause price to break out over resistance. The next week, price reversed lower with a long black candle that caused the RSI to retreat also, leaving its overhead resistance intact.

Coming into the point E low, a number of inverted hammers and spinning tops and one doji formed as volume declined. This was an indication that sellers were losing their conviction and that a downside breakout of the range was now a low-probability event. Price found support in the vicinity of the point A low, and the RSI confirmed by finding support in the same area. After the formation of the doji at point E, price reversed higher with a series of white candles on increasing volume. This showed that the conviction of buyers was increasing and that an upside breakout of the range was likely. Remember, the sharp move higher off the low took place over a three-week period before the breakout, which gave traders and chart scanners plenty of time to analyze and track this situation and prepare to place a trade. Price finally broke up through resistance in October 2006 with a long white candle, which triggered a long trade. A protective sell stop order could have been placed just below the point D high as what was once resistance now became support. If price retreated back into the range, that would have been deemed a false breakout, thus negating the reason for taking the trade. Placing the stop just below that point would eliminate any rationalization for holding the trade. Once the reason for taking the trade no longer exists, it is time to get out.

If you look at the plot of the RSI, you will notice that the RSI actually broke up through its resistance line one week before price, telegraphing the price breakout. This showed that momentum was finally strong enough for price to break out over the resistance formed by the falling window and price highs at points B and D. This example once again proves that the weight of the evidence method is sound as the confluence of support and resistance, momentum, volume, and candlestick lines and patterns confirmed one another. Trading with a confluence of indicators requires discipline and patience, but the results are well worth the time invested.

TRADER'S MENTAL CHECKLIST

The three examples above are meant to get you started in your trading analysis by showing you what to look for and how to exploit trading situations as they arise. Developing your understanding of the necessary analysis tools is only half the battle, however. The most difficult part of trading is knowing how to prepare and react *mentally* to situations as they develop. In today's world of the Internet and electronic trading, it is imperative that traders not get caught up in the endless stream of hype, news, and the opinions of others. Below is a checklist of six items that traders must be conscious of to make sure they are taking a trade for the right reasons instead of giving in to the emotions and will of the masses.

1. **Guard against fear and greed.** Do not enter a trade simply because you are afraid of missing an opportunity. Are you entering a trade because others are making money in that trade? Always assess what is and do not get caught up in the success of others. Do not exit a trade because you are fearful of losses; exit only if you decide to take a profit or if your stop loss is triggered (see point 6, below).

2. **Be patient.** If you see a trade setting up but do not have price confirmation (such as a confirmed trend continuation or reversal) yet, wait for price confirmation before entering the trade. *Assuming* that a pattern will resolve itself in a particular way without price confirmation can lead to unnecessary losses.

3. **Always be detached from the emotion of the market.** Watching CNBC and other all-day market news sources can get you caught up in intraday hype, and that can cause you to make trades on the basis of emotion rather than sound analysis. Also be careful of reading too many news stories that can slant your market opinion. There were many doubters of the market after the 2009 low because the news was still very pessimistic even though the market was rallying sharply. Those who shorted the market during that time because of the news stories and/ or their own opinions probably are now working in other industries or capacities.

4. **The market is never wrong.** Even if you don't agree with the reasons for a market advance or decline, pay attention and let your charts guide you. The market doesn't care about your opinion, and market action is the collective will of *all* traders. If your analysis does not coincide with

what the market is doing, step aside and wait for things to become clearer.

5. **Be unwavering in your execution.** When your analysis says it is time to execute a trade, jump in and execute. Don't be a handwringer who looks for excuses for not making trades. If you use a weight of the evidence methodology, there are multiple layers lining up to say that the trade is a go. Do not doubt them.

6. **Always use stops.** This is paramount. You will not get every trade right no matter how sound and thorough your analysis is. Stops prevent traders from turning what was meant to be a short-term trade into a buy and hope position. Wall Street is filled with buy and hopers who only know how to buy and hold on for the ride with white knuckles. They are a dime a dozen. Use your own rules and be disciplined. Set your stops at places where when they are hit, the reason for taking the trade no longer exists (e.g., a breakout that has failed). Stops are a way for traders to control their personal trading risk and avoid devastating losses.

SUMMARY

The foundation for a solid trading system can be developed by using a weight of the evidence methodology. By assembling pieces that confirm each other, a trader can increase the odds of making successful trades. Using candlesticks with trend analysis, support and resistance, momentum indicators, and volume can provide a complete picture of the mindset of traders that should reveal to a trader what is likely to occur. Once price has confirmed the identified scenario by either reversing or continuing the trend, a trade can be executed with confidence. Never forget to use stops, however, as market risk is always present and must be addressed. The technical aspect of trading consists of the messages given by chart analysis. The mental aspect also must be considered to keep a trader from being swayed by emotion or the opinions of others. Mastering the technical and mental aspects in tandem will greatly increase the odds of becoming a successful trader.

PART 3

Candlestick Cousins: Other Charting Methods

CHAPTER 9

Three-Line Break Charts

Three-line break charts get their name from the number of boxes, or *lines*, needed to cause a price trend reversal. Three-line break charts are similar to point and figure charts (Chapter 1) because they ignore the passage of time and do not use volume. New lines are drawn on the chart only when certain prior closing price levels are exceeded regardless of how long it took price to reach that level. This charting method originated in Japan and was introduced to Western technical analysis by Steve Nison. This chapter will cover the basics and suggested uses of three-line break charts. It will be up to you to apply yourself to mastering this charting style if you choose to do so. Being a successful trader takes hard work. Developing a deeper understanding of the markets and the tools available to you will put you well ahead of the many traders who attempt to succeed with minimal effort.

A three-line break chart appears as a series of white and black boxes that move up and down, depending on the direction in which price is trending. Although three-line break charts are similar to point and figure charts in that a time element is not relevant to their construction, they differ in that they use only the closing price, whereas point and figure charts use high and low prices to determine when a new box is to be drawn. Another difference is that new lines are drawn on three-line break charts when a new closing high or low is made, not at a predetermined amount chosen by the chartist.

New lines are drawn on the chart when the current close exceeds the previous closing high or when the current closing price is lower than the previous closing low. New white lines are added as price moves higher, and new black lines are added as price moves lower. The following guidelines are used in adding new lines to a three-line break chart:

- A new white line is drawn when the closing price exceeds the previous line's high price.
- A new black line is drawn when the closing price is lower than the previous bar's low price.
- Nothing is drawn if the closing price is not outside the range of the previous bar.

There are basic trading rules for trading three-line break charts:

- Buy when a white turnaround line is drawn after three consecutive black lines.
- Sell when a black line is drawn after three consecutive white lines.
- Avoid trendless or whipsaw markets in which lines alternate between black and white.

Figure 9-1 illustrates how new lines would be added to a three-line break chart in a trending market.

THREE-LINE BREAK TRENDS

The daily chart of IBM in Figure 9-2 shows how the lines appear on an actual chart. Note the series of white or hollow lines that show a strong uptrend. When you are choosing your time frame, that makes a difference in the appearance of the chart. Do not be confused by the lack of a uniform time axis on the chart itself. In plotting a daily time frame, daily data are used. In plotting a weekly time frame, weekly data are used. This means that in the weekly time frame, the closing price for each week (one single price) is used instead of using the five daily closing prices over the same time frame. The

FIGURE 9-1

New Lines in a Three-Line Break Chart

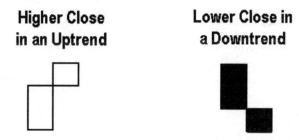

Higher Close in an Uptrend

Lower Close in a Downtrend

difference in time frame selection can give the chart a different look, just as in daily and weekly candlestick charts.

After examining Figure 9-2, take a look at Figure 9-3, which is the same IBM chart displayed using weekly data. The weekly

FIGURE 9-2

Three-Line Break for IBM, Daily

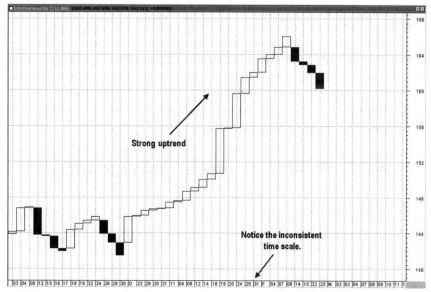

Source: MetaStock

FIGURE 9-3

Three-Line Break for IBM, Weekly

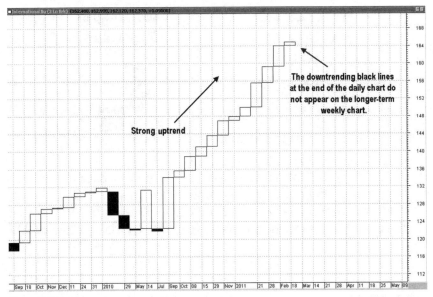

Source: MetaStock

chart has a cleaner look with fewer intermittent trend reversals. This could make the weekly chart more appealing for longer-term trend traders. Using weekly data allows a trader to stay with the trend longer, but a price is paid in the form of the amount of price movement that is required before a reversal signal is generated as Figure 9-2 and Figure 9-3 illustrate.

THREE-LINE BREAK TREND REVERSALS

The strength of the three-line break charting method lies in its ability to display the price trend. A series of consecutive white lines shows that the market is making higher highs, and a series of consecutive black lines shows that the market is making lower lows. What does it take, however, for a white line to change to black and vice versa? First, a reversal can occur from white to black when a new low is made for the move; that occurs when price closes below the low of the first white bar of the move higher. The same thing occurs in a reversal from a black line to a white line when price makes a new high for the move. These instances occur early in price moves before a new trend is established by forming at least three consecutive lines in the same direction. Figure 9-4 shows reversals early in price moves.

The second way a reversal is plotted gives the three-line break charting method its name. This method requires a trending market that is strong enough to post at least three consecutive lines of the same color. A downside reversal (white line changing to black) occurs when the price closes under the lowest of the last three consecutive white blocks. The new black line is drawn from the bottom of the highest white line down to the new closing price. An upside reversal (black line changing to white) occurs when the price closes above the highest price of the most recent three consecutive black lines. The new white line is drawn from the top of the lowest black line to the new closing price. Figure 9-5 shows three-line break reversals.

FIGURE 9-4

Line Break Reversals

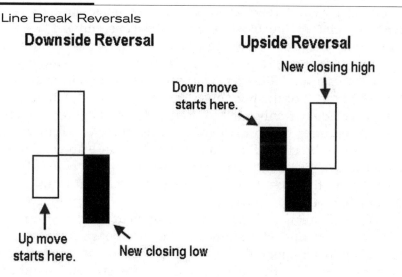

FIGURE 9-5

Three-Line Break Reversals

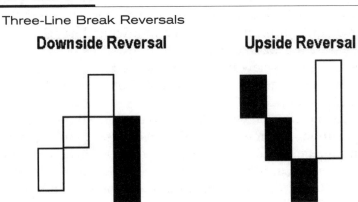

It is important to understand the two types of reversals and how they occur. The daily chart of Applied Materials, Inc., in Figure 9-6 shows some good reversal examples. The first two examples are three-line break reversals. These reversals occur when there are at least three lines of the same color in the direction of the trend (three consecutive black lines or three consecutive white lines). For a reversal to occur, price must close above the highest point of the most recent three consecutive black lines (upside reversal) or below the low of the most recent three consecutive white lines (downside reversal). The final example on the chart shows a single-line reversal. A black line was formed on the three-line break of the previous three consecutive white lines but was reversed after only one box. Remember that a three-line break reversal requires the formation of at least three consecutive lines in the same direction. Prior to that point, a close above the most recent one or two black lines can cause an upside reversal and a close below the most recent one or two white lines can cause a downside reversal.

One advantage of three-line break charts is that it does not take an arbitrarily set amount of points to constitute a reversal. It is price action alone that gives an indication of a reversal, not settings chosen by the chartist, such as box size and number of

FIGURE 9-6

Three-Line Break Reversals for Applied Materials, Inc., Daily

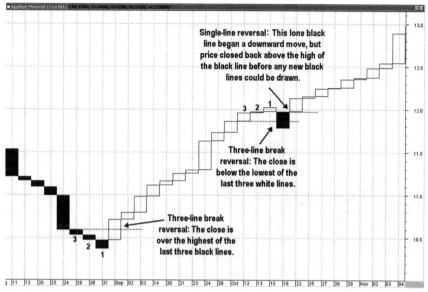

Source: MetaStock

boxes with the point and figure method. One disadvantage is that when a reversal does occur, the new trend in many cases is well under way, which can make trading the reversal riskier because the trade is being entered farther away from a possible stop point at a previous high or low. There is a way to alleviate the late reversal signal issue partially, however. When three-line break charts are used in conjunction with candlestick charts, easing into longer-term positions in two stages is a viable option. For example, on a normal candlestick reversal the trader would initiate half of a position, with the other half being added later, once the three-line break chart confirms the reversal. Using this approach requires that a candlestick reversal "prove" itself with a meaningful three-line break reversal before a full position is taken.

To illustrate this point, take a look at a three-line break chart of IBM in Figure 9-7 with the focus on the September 24, 2010, reversal that kicked off a strong rally. If a trader had been using

FIGURE 9-7

Upside Reversal for IBM, Daily

Source: MetaStock

only the three-line break chart, the September 24 buy signal would have occurred well above support, which would have resulted in the protective sell stop being placed over 8 percent below the buy point.

When a daily candlestick chart of IBM is included, however, Figure 9-8 shows that an earlier entry is possible, allowing for a smaller distance between the buy price and the stop price. This is also a more conservative way to build a position as the three-line break reversal signal must occur to put on the second half of the position. To put on the first half of the position, we will use the weight of the evidence approach that gave clues that a reversal was occurring. Figure 9-8 consists of the price plot of IBM with a 14-period RSI and a plot of volume. When you look at the chart, notice the following:

1. The decline into the early September low allowed for a resistance line to be drawn that when broken would be used as a buy signal.

FIGURE 9-8

Trend Reversal Buy for IBM, Daily

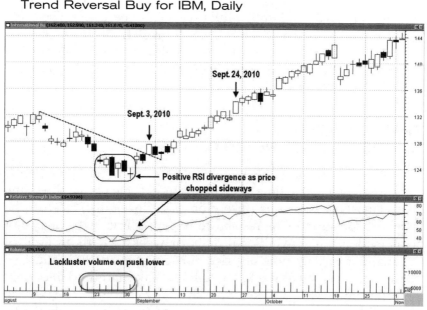

Source: MetaStock

2. Volume heading into the early September low was weak, which showed a lack of conviction among sellers.

3. The RSI showed a positive divergence, as it made a higher low as price chopped sideways to lower from August 26 to August 31.

4. The candle that formed on August 31 (the last candle inside the circled area) was a low-volume doji, which again showed a lack of conviction among sellers.

5. A white candle broke the downward-sloping resistance line on September 3, which triggered the initial buy at 127.58 with a stop placement below the August 31 doji low of 122.28. This provided much more favorable risk exposure of around 2 percent from entry price to stop.

The second buy came much later, on September 24, after the three-line break signal was given. This shows how late three-line break signals can be, but by combining two different methodologies, longer-term traders can build partial positions earlier, which allows them to participate in early trend changes but commit less capital until a full reversal has occurred. The trade in Figure 9-8 also would have been a great trade for a shorter-term trader, but by using three-line break charts, even short-term traders can allow their successful positions to turn into longer-term holds if they choose.

THREE-LINE BREAK
SUPPORT AND RESISTANCE

Three-line break charts also show support and resistance points very well. Since the time element is not a factor on three-line break charts, the focus is purely on price levels that need to be breached for support or resistance to fail. These levels may not be as evident on conventional daily or weekly charts in light of the fact that for any type of price movement, something must be plotted for each day or week. Three-line break charts add lines only if a prior high or low is taken out. The daily chart of F5 Networks, Inc., in Figure 9-9 shows how support and resistance levels can be observed more easily without the obligation to post a new price in every single time period.

The breakout at point A was significant in that it broke three separate resistance lines at the same time. It broke the horizontal resistance lines drawn off the two previous highs as well as the downsloping resistance line that capped any rally attempts as price moved lower. After the break of the resistance lines and the beginning of a new uptrend, new resistance lines were drawn each time price reversed lower at points B, C, and D. In each case, the resistance line was broken to the upside, which showed the strength of the uptrend. Using three-line breaks to identify breakouts over resistance allows a trader to add positions in an uptrend similar to the trading methodology discussed in Chapter 8.

Another example of support and resistance is shown in the daily chart of the CRB (Commodity Research Bureau) Index in Figure 9-10. This is used more as a market analysis example as the CRB Index is a tracking index for commodity prices. Three separate lines are drawn on the chart. Lines A and B represent support, and line C represents resistance. Line A provided support for prices as they declined, defining zones where commodity prices could be

FIGURE 9-9

Support and Resistance for F5 Networks, Inc., Daily

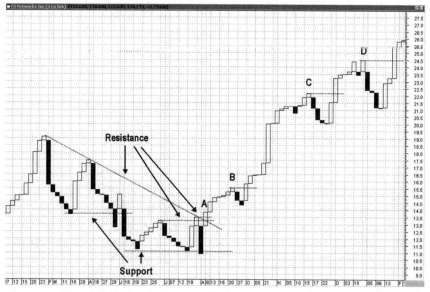

Source: MetaStock

FIGURE 9-10

Support and Resistance for CRB Index, Daily

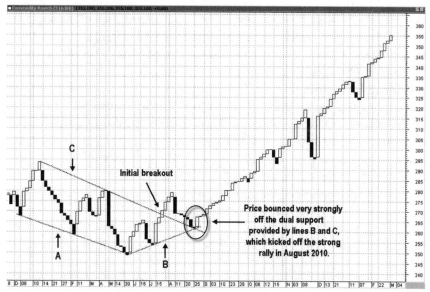

Source: MetaStock

expected to bounce. Support line B was drawn between the May 2010 price low and the first pullback low in July as commodity prices began to rally. This was now a line that would be expected to provide support for commodity prices as a new uptrend was trying to develop. Line C was resistance drawn off the January 2010 reactionary high. This resistance line kept a cap on any rally attempts into the May low.

As the CRB Index began to move higher, line C was a very important one to watch. Price finally broke above resistance line C in July, but pulled back soon afterward to a point that was below the breakout point. This may have caused some to believe that the rally in commodities was over for the time being, but those who carried their trendlines farther across the chart knew differently. Remember the adage from Chapter 5: What was once resistance is now support. Price pulled back into the extended resistance line C and also was supported by upsloping support line B. This provided dual support, at which point price reversed higher, kicking off the furious commodity rally that was still strong in spring 2011. Dual support or resistance areas like this are very strong. For this reason it always pays to extend older trendlines on your charts because you never know when they may come into play again.

THREE-LINE BREAK AND WINDOWS

As was discussed in Chapter 5, one important aspect of support and resistance in candlestick charting is the formation of windows (gaps). Since three-line break charts do not use the other three price elements used in candlestick charting (open, high, and low), the formation of rising or falling windows is not possible. Note in the daily candlestick chart of Amazon.com in Figure 9-11 how the rising window that formed in October 2009 on the left side of the chart was solid support that enabled Amazon to rally to new highs. The shaded area from 100 to 110 was closed only partially in July 2010 before price reversed sharply higher.

Take a look at a three-line break chart of Amazon.com in Figure 9-12 with the same price range shaded. Notice that where the rising window occurred, there is only a long white line since only the closing price was used. There is no evidence of the support that was provided by the rising window shown in Figure 9-11. In fact, the break of support (into the shaded area around $110) on the

FIGURE 9-11

Rising Window for Amazon.com, Daily

Source: MetaStock

FIGURE 9-12

Three-Line Break, No Window, for Amazon.com, Daily

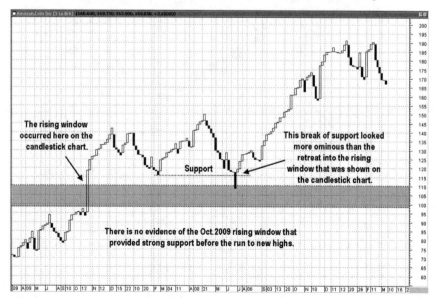

Source: MetaStock

three-line break looked worse than it did on the candlestick chart because evidence of the rising window as support was not present.

THREE-LINE BREAK AS A TREND FILTER

The larger degree trend picture painted by a three-line break chart makes it a valuable tool to use as a filter during the decision process on the likelihood of a candlestick chart reversal or continuation pattern being successful. This method is definitely not foolproof, and this is why stops should be used on every trade, regardless of the situation. This is another tool, however, that can tilt the odds of success in your favor as trades are either taken or bypassed, depending on the larger degree trend. The chart of Intel Corporation in Figure 9-13 shows positive and negative periods for the stock. Intel was in a positive or uptrending phase from October 22 through December 10, 2010. The uptrend reversed,

FIGURE 9-13

Three-Line Break Trend for Intel Corporation, Daily

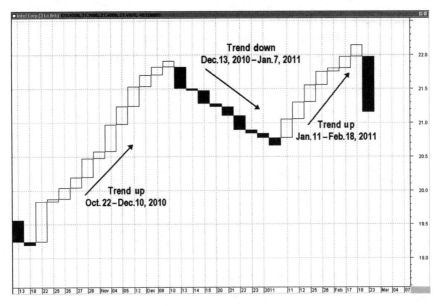

Source: MetaStock

which ushered in a period of weakness from December 13, 2010, through January 7, 2011. Finally, another uptrend was in effect from January 11 through February 18, 2011. During these periods, any reversal pattern against the prevailing trend should be viewed as somewhat suspect, whereas continuation patterns should be viewed with a higher degree of certainty. These trend concepts were covered in Chapter 5, and this is simply another way to display the prevailing trend.

The daily chart of Intel in candlestick format in Figure 9-14 covers the uptrending period between October 22 and December 10, 2010. Three points are marked A, B, and C. Points A and C are both bearish engulfing patterns, which are normally very strong reversal signals, but the occurrence at point A was followed immediately by a white candle and a resumption of the uptrend, and the occurrence at point C was followed by a series of spinning tops with no further downside price movement. These are prime

FIGURE 9-14

Candlestick Reversal Patterns against the Trend for Intel, Daily

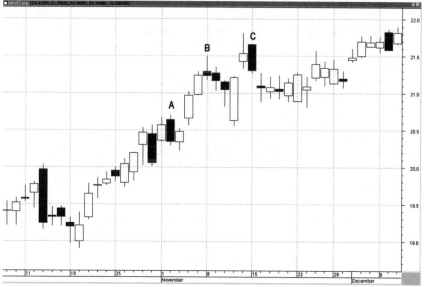

Source: MetaStock

examples of trend strength being driven by the demand of buyers. This demand puts a floor under prices, preventing deeper declines. Point B was a shooting star or inverted hammer that was followed by a spinning top and a hammer, hardly an inspiration to the bears. These normally strong reversal signals all had one thing in common: no follow-through selling. In this case the strength shown by the three-line break chart could have been a valuable filter to help assess the trading landscape.

THREE-LINE BREAK AND TREND MOMENTUM

The construction of three-line break charts also allows for a quick assessment of trend momentum. As a healthy trend is in force in a three-line break chart, the lines are usually longer, showing good strength and conviction among traders as they push the price either higher or lower. The daily chart of D.R. Horton, Inc., in Figure 9-15 illustrates how shorter lines preceded reversals in the opposite direction (circled areas). Not every short line in the direction of the trend results in a reversal, and so it is wise to wait for a reversal before committing to the other direction with any new trades. Take a look at the downtrend on the left side of the chart and the uptrend on the right side. Each of those trends contained short lines, but they were followed immediately by continuations in the same direction. The center portion of the chart is choppy and range-bound, which is a better environment for momentum loss to lead to a reversal as buyers and sellers battle to establish control of the larger degree trend.

The concept of the smaller lines is the same as with candlesticks and the theories behind the spinning top, doji, inverted hammer, and hanging man. Their small real bodies show a struggle for control of price direction. Each of these reliable patterns still needs some form of confirmation (reversal) before being deemed successful. The odds of a reversal in direction increase on a three-line break chart when shoes, suits, and necks appear.

SHOES, SUITS, AND NECKS

The colorful pattern descriptions used by the Japanese also have a place in three-line break charting. Just as the hanging man,

FIGURE 9-15

Trend Momentum for D.R. Horton, Inc., Daily

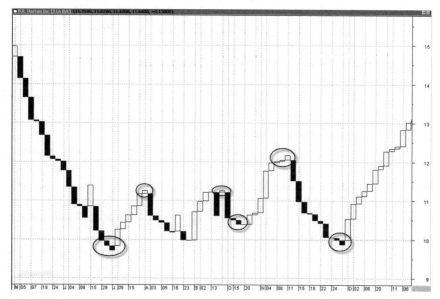

Source: MetaStock

hammer, dark cloud cover, and so forth, are recognizable lines and patterns in candlestick charting, shoes, suits, and necks form three step reversal patterns in three-line break charting. Shoes typically appear as very short lines in the direction of the trend. A shoe alerts a trader that trend momentum may be waning and that a change in price direction may be near. A white shoe shows slowing momentum in an uptrend, and a black shoe shows slowing momentum in a downtrend. A suit is the long opposite-colored line that follows a shoe. For example, a white shoe is followed by a black suit and a black shoe is followed by a white suit. A neck is typically a shorter line after the suit that confirms the reversal. Necks get their name because the line resembles a neck coming out of the top of a suit. This reversal pattern appears in the following sequence:

1. A shoe forms in the direction of the trend: a black shoe in a downtrend or a white shoe in an uptrend.
2. Price reverses with a long line of the opposite color. This is the suit. A white suit follows a black shoe, and a black suit follows a white shoe.

3. A new, shorter line is formed in the direction of the trend, confirming the reversal. This is the neck.

The daily chart of the Nasdaq Composite Index in Figure 9-16 shows three consecutive reversals that contain shoes, suits, and necks. The first and third reversals are upside reversals started with a black shoe followed by a white suit and neck. The second reversal is a downside reversal started with a white shoe followed by a black suit and neck. These patterns are effective on the market indexes and can contribute to broad market analysis in addition to analysis of individual securities.

If you take a closer look at Figure 9-14, you will see that between the first and second reversals there is what looks to be a white shoe followed by a black suit. The absence of a neck line following the black suit meant that the reversal was not confirmed. Note that the downside reversal lasted only one line before reversing back to the upside.

FIGURE 9-16

Shoes, Suits, and Necks for Nasdaq Composite Index, Daily

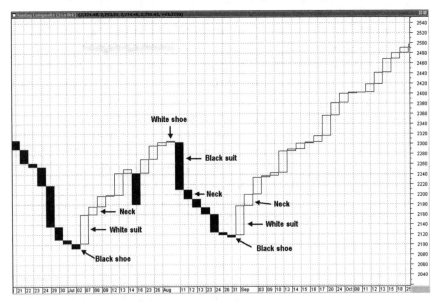

Source: MetaStock

TWO-, THREE-, AND FOUR-LINE BREAKS

Although the number three is the most commonly used in break charts (three-line break), other values can be used as well. For example, a two-line break chart can be constructed for shorter-term traders who want to trade the markets more frequently. A four-line break chart can be used by longer-term traders who want to ride trends for longer periods before signals in the opposite direction are given. These charts work the same way as three-line break charts with regard to reversal rules at the beginning of price moves. On a two-line break chart, only two lines are required for a two-line break reversal; on a four-line break chart, four lines in a row are required for a four-line break reversal. A two-line break chart will produce more frequent and less reliable signals, and a four-line break will produce fewer signals, but those signals will come later, after a new trend has been established. The daily chart of Netflix, Inc., in Figure 9-17 shows a comparison of two-, three-, and four-line break charts.

FIGURE 9-17

Two-, Three-, and Four-Line Break Charts for Netflix, Inc., Daily

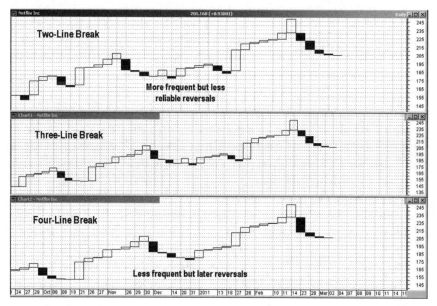

Source: MetaStock

SUMMARY

Three-line break charting is a method that is purely price driven with no regard for a time component. The advantage of using this charting method is that new lines are drawn only when price makes a new high or low, which eliminates noise or insignificant price movement. The strengths of three-line break charts are as follows:

- They are very effective in showing the prevailing trend.
- They reveal important support and resistance levels.
- They demonstrate when trend momentum may be waning.

The disadvantages of using this charting method are as follows:

- Once a reversal occurs, the new trend is typically well under way, causing late entry.
- Volume is not used.
- Windows or gaps are not evident on the chart.

The issue of later trend entry can be alleviated partially by using three-line break charts in conjunction with standard candlestick charts. When a trader takes half positions on candlestick reversals and applies the other half on the three-line break chart once the reversal is confirmed, a lower-risk entry point can be established for longer-term traders. Three-line break charts can take on different looks with regard to the trend, depending on the type of data used (daily, weekly, etc.). Reversals in price direction can occur either just after a new price move has begun or after a trend has been in force in the form of three or more lines forming in the same direction. Three-line break charts provide a quick assessment of the trend, support and resistance levels, and whether the odds have increased for a reversal of trend. By using a three-line break chart to assess the trend, a trader can employ it as a filter to get a better idea about whether to take countertrend trades. Break charts can be used with the two or four lines instead of three, depending on one's trading preference, but two-line break charts produce more frequent, less reliable signals, whereas four-line break charts produce less frequent, later signals.

CHAPTER 10

Renko Charts

Like the three-line break, renko is a charting method that uses only the closing price, does not have a uniform time axis, does not use volume, and does not reveal windows or gaps. The word renko comes from the Japanese word *renga*, which means "brick." A renko chart more closely resembles a point and figure chart than a three-line break chart in its construction. Recall that a three-line break chart moves purely on price action in relation to prior highs and lows. A renko chart, in contrast, does not move until a threshold or minimum price move has occurred that is set by the chartist. In many charting packages the minimum price move that the chartist sets is referred to as the reversal amount. I don't like that term because not every violation of that amount results in a reversal. In many cases it results in a new brick being drawn in the direction of the prevailing trend.

Whereas point and figure charts use the high and low prices for each session, a renko chart only uses the closing price. Trading signals are generated when a new white or hollow brick appears after a black brick (buy signal) or when a new black brick appears after a white brick (sell signal). Just like three-line break charts, renko charts are great at filtering out noise or insignificant price fluctuations as well as showing the overall price trend and support and resistance levels. Figure 10-1 shows a renko chart.

FIGURE 10-1

Renko Chart Example

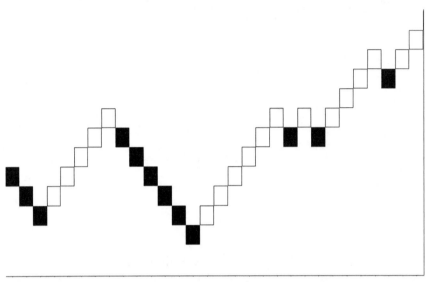

Source: MetaStock

CONSTRUCTING A RENKO CHART

The construction of a renko chart is simple but can be confusing at first. A new brick is not added unless it is enough points away from the reference point. For example, if the brick size is set to two points and the starting point was 10, a price move from 10 to 12 on a closing basis would mean that a new white brick should be added. Table 10-1 illustrates the basics, using 10 as the starting point. The "Price" column represents the closing price for the day, and the "New Brick?" column will contain +1 if a new white brick is added to the upside and –1 if a new black brick is added to the downside.

In Table 10-1, you can see the math involved in adding new bricks to the chart. If we start at a reference point of 10, it will take a close at or above 12 to add a new white brick (+1) or a close at or below 8 to add a new black brick (–1). Until either of those two prices is met, nothing is drawn. On day 5, price moved higher to 12, and so a new white brick was added (+1). This means now that

TABLE 10-1

Renko Chart Calculation—2 Point Brick Size

Day	Price	New Brick?	Day	Price	New Brick?
1	10.00		13	14.00	
2	11.25		14	14.25	
3	10.75		15	12.25	
4	11.75		16	13.35	
5	12.00	+1	17	12.10	
6	11.50		18	11.95	−1
7	13.50		19	11.50	
8	13.75		20	10.25	
9	14.10	+1	21	9.75	−1
10	15.00		22	11.75	
11	15.25		23	11.35	
12	16.05	+1	24	12.08	

our new thresholds are 14 for a new brick to be added to the upside (+1) and 8 for a new black brick to be added to the downside (−1). When one is plotting reversal bricks, they are added to the chart when price is 2 points beyond the extreme of the most recent brick in the opposite direction. For example, if the latest brick is drawn from 10 to 12 (2 points), a reversal lower cannot occur until price declines to 8, which is 2 points below 10 (the low of the most recent brick).

On day 9 price exceeded 14, closing at 14.10. The new brick is drawn from 12 to 14. The extra .10 over 14 is ignored as bricks are plotted only in 2-point increments. Now our new thresholds are 16 to the upside and 10 to the downside. On day 12, price closed at 16.05, which is above 16, and so a new brick is added from 14 to 16. This makes our new thresholds 18 and 12. After the high of 16.05 on day 12, price began a decline. Remember, however, that a new downside brick cannot be added until price closes at least 2 points *below the low* of the most recent brick. On day 18, price closed at 11.95, which is below 12, and so a new downside brick (−1) is added and drawn from 14 to 12. Our new thresholds are 16 and 10. On day 21, price closed at 9.75, which was below the threshold of 10, and so a new downside brick is drawn from 12 down to 10. This leaves our new thresholds at 14 and 8. It is also possible for more than one brick to be added at a time if price exceeds the value of the next two thresholds. For example, if our upside threshold was 12 and price jumped from 10 to 15, not only would a brick be drawn from 10 to 12, a brick would be drawn from 12 to 14 as well.

It is also important to note that when you are constructing a renko chart, you must not confuse daily price moves with the threshold values needed to add another brick. If price jumps two points in one day, nothing is drawn unless that two-point move results in the breach of a threshold value. For example, if the latest brick drawn was a white brick from 10 to 12 and price moved from 11.95 to 13.95, no brick would be drawn since price did not close at or above 14 (12 + 2).

RENKO CHARTS AND TRENDS

Renko charts can be used to identify trends as the contrasting colors of the bricks make uptrends and downtrends stand out. A trend reversal is signaled by a change in color from a white brick to a black brick and vice versa. The two-point daily chart of Vail Resorts, Inc., in Figure 10-2 shows how the black brick and the pattern of lower highs and lower lows mark the downtrend on the left side of the chart. After the reversal at the bottom of the chart, a new uptrend began, demonstrated by the pattern of higher highs and higher lows along with the predominance of white bricks. This is another great example of the wisdom of trading with the trend as the countertrend moves did not last for very long, especially in the new uptrend after the reversal higher. Note how few black bricks there are on the right side of the chart.

Also note that the downtrend in Figure 10-2 has a choppy appearance, with numerous countertrend reversals along the way. These brief changes in direction signified changes in shorter-term momentum, whereas the larger degree trend (lower highs and lower lows) remained intact. When it comes to renko charts and trends, setting the brick size to a smaller number results in more sensitivity to price reversals but typically also results in a choppier

FIGURE 10-2

Renko Chart Trend for Vail Resorts, Inc., Daily

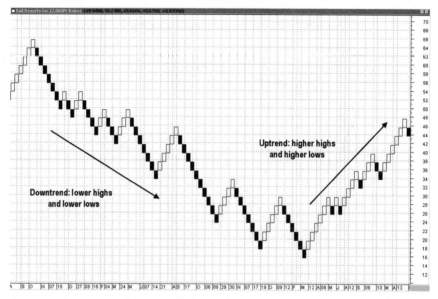

Source: MetaStock

appearance. Setting the brick size to a larger number, however, results in fewer but more meaningful reversal signals. The price to be paid for fewer, more reliable signals is that it takes a larger price move to generate a reversal signal, and this results in later trade entry once a new trend has begun.

RENKO CHARTS AND SUPPORT AND RESISTANCE

Renko charts can be used to identify key support and resistance zones, and this can aid trading decisions. Tightly clustered blocks easily identify consolidation areas that can provide good trading opportunities on breakouts. Support and resistance also can be used to validate the strength of price trends. The daily two-point chart of SanDisk Corporation in Figure 10-3 shows examples of support and resistance.

FIGURE 10-3

Renko Support and Resistance for SanDisk Corporation,
Daily

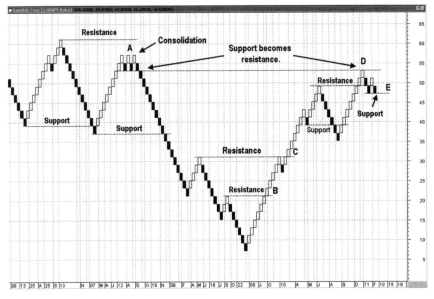

On the left side of the chart, notice the horizontal line drawn
off the high just over 60, which would become resistance later on.
After the initial decline to between 35 and 40, price rebounded into
point A, where it challenged the previous high just over 60. Before
price could get up into that resistance level, however, it began a
consolidation phase as SanDisk chopped sideways between 54 and
58. Consolidation just below a previous high could be new accumulation before a push to new highs or could be distribution at
resistance. A trader's ability to figure out the intentions of traders
is handicapped without candlesticks and volume to work with,
and so in using renko charts it is prudent to wait patiently for
the breakout to enter a trade. Our first point of reference is the
downside breakout of consolidation at point A, which led to a nice
short trading opportunity. Trading back and forth in the consolidation period at point A as the bricks shifted from white to black

and back would have created frustration and losses as the signals whipsawed back and forth. In this case, patiently waiting for a meaningful support level to be breached would have led to a better trading opportunity.

After the breakdown through support, SanDisk Corporation was in a ferocious downtrend all the way to the bottom between 5 and 10. Buying SanDisk on the first white brick off the low would have been a risky proposition since the previous two reversal attempts were followed by a resumption of the downtrend. One way to mitigate the risk in this case would have been to wait for a break of prior resistance that showed that buyers were taking control of the trend. Doing so would have meant getting in much later at point B as price moved above 20, but it was well worth the wait as the new trend continued sharply higher. Another resistance level just above 30 was penetrated at point C as the uptrend gained steam, which further demonstrated the resolve of buyers.

After a spirited correction that took SanDisk from just under 50 to the 35 area, price climbed higher into point D. Notice at point D how price encountered resistance that was formed by the bottom of the consolidation area at point A (former support). This reinforces the rule that prior support becomes resistance. Price then sold off slightly at point D, where a new consolidation/support area appears to be forming at point E. At the time of this writing, this pattern is unresolved, and without volume and candlesticks it is more difficult to see what traders are doing here. However, if history repeats itself, we have a consolidation just below resistance just as we had at point A. This would lead me to believe that this is distribution and that a downside breakout can be expected. As was stated earlier, however, it is always wise to wait for price to break either support or resistance before placing any trades regardless of how strongly you feel about which way price *might* break.

As was mentioned earlier, changing the point value of a renko chart can change its look. Figure 10-4 is a three-point chart of SanDisk Corporation over the exact same time frame. Notice how the consolidation phase at point A in Figure 10-3 is no longer present and the two support areas on the left side of the chart before the decline into the major low are in a straight line. The break of support in Figure 10-4 was a more ominous sign than the breaks of individual support areas on the way down in Figure 10-3.

FIGURE 10-4

Renko Three-Point Chart for SanDisk Corporation, Daily

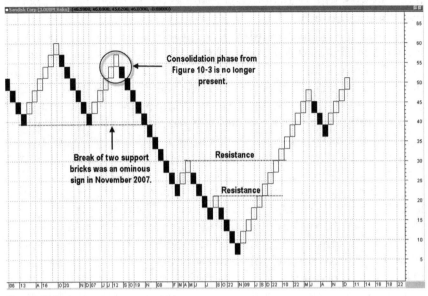

Source: MetaStock

Look again at the chart of SanDisk Corporation over the same time period, this time using the four-point brick setting in Figure 10-5. Notice how this setting removes the first resistance (at just over 20) off the low.

SETTING THE BRICK SIZE

In the examples shown so far, the brick sizes have been set to acceptable levels for most individual stocks. These are practical settings for many charts, but what about setting the box size for a chart of the Dow Jones Industrial Average, for example? The Dow can move two points in nanoseconds, and so a setting of 2 would be impractical. At the other end of the spectrum, a two-point setting is also not practical on a $5 stock as a move of 40 percent would have to occur to draw a new brick. What should one do in these cases?

FIGURE 10-5

Renko Four-Point Chart for SanDisk Corporation, Daily

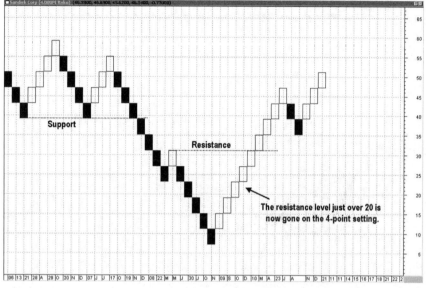

Source: MetaStock

One school of thought is to adjust the brick size on the basis of the Average True Range of the recent price action. Average True Range is an indicator developed by J. Welles Wilder to capture the true volatility of a security or commodity. Without getting too far into its actual computation, the average of true ranges over a period is computed. The default value in this case is typically 14 trading bars. Most charting software will compute this value for you. The drawback to using this method is that Average True Range values can fluctuate greatly during periods of increased volatility, and that affects the setting of the brick size. For example, if the brick size is set during a period of high volatility, it may be as high as five or six, whereas during normal periods, it may be two or three. As was demonstrated above, a mere one-point difference in brick size can alter the chart's appearance.

Another method (and the one I prefer) is to base the brick size on the price scale of the stock or commodity one wants to chart. This is done by dividing the price of the security by 20 and

FIGURE 10-6

Renko Chart with 200-Point Brick Size for Dow Jones
Industrial Average

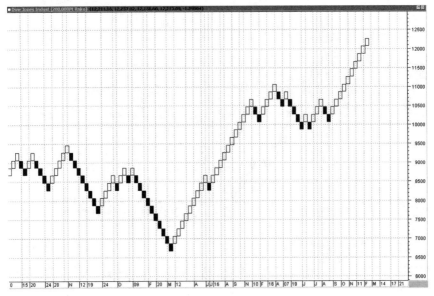

Source: MetaStock

rounding down to the nearest whole number. This means that any
stock, for example, that is priced under 40 would have a brick size
of 1, a stock priced above 40 but under 60 would have a brick size
of 2, a stock priced at 60 or above but below 80 would have a brick
size of 3, and so on. For stocks below $20, divide by 20 and round
down to the nearest .05. That means that a $3.50 stock should have
the brick size set to .15 (3.50/20 = .175, rounded to .15). As for the
indexes, I prefer to use set values of 200 for the Dow and 20 for the
S&P 500. These are merely guidelines to get you started setting up
and using renko charts. For example, if you prefer a brick size of 2
on an $80 stock, that is acceptable if you are getting good signals
and are comfortable with those settings. The method you use to set
your brick size is totally up to you.

The chart of the Dow Jones Industrial Average in Figure 10-6
shows how the chart would look with a brick setting of 200.

CAUTIONARY NOTE

A word of caution is in order here with regard to trading renko charts. Although the trades may look like nice winners in many cases, appearances can be deceiving. Remember that for a reversal to occur on a two-point chart, a four-point move must occur. That means that four points of a possible new trend have been given up before a trade is entered. The issue becomes even more acute if the reversal turns out to be nothing more than a brief countertrend bounce.

Renko charts also do not show the exact point where price closed. For example, if price has reversed to the upside to the point where a new box is drawn, where did the price actually close? If the reversal necessitated the drawing of a new brick from 48 to 50, price could have closed anywhere from 50 to 51.99. If you made a trade there, you obviously would know your entry price, but the point of this brief discussion is not to take a glance at a renko chart and see three or four white bricks in a row and assume that the trade would have been a solid winner. If you were holding a long position until a reversal lower occurred on a two-point scale, the trade would not be exited until a four-point reversal lower had occurred. If price had reversed lower from a high of 54, that means a new black brick would be drawn from 48 to 50, which means that the actual close could have been anywhere from 46.01 to 48.00.

The chart of KLA-Tencor Corporation in Figure 10-7 illustrates how trading what turns out to be a countertrend bounce can end up as a losing trade. The top of the brick that gave the entry signal was 40.60, and the bottom of the brick that gave the exit signal was also 40.60. It is highly unlikely that the trade entry and exit were at the very best possible prices in each case. Shorting KLA-Tencor following these brief countertrend bounces would have been very profitable as KLA-Tencor Corporation was in a strong downtrend, as shown by the large number of consecutive black bricks.

Although a long string of consecutive bricks of the same color is an obvious big winner if traded at the reversal point, the smaller countertrend and whipsaw reversals are not as attractive as they appear on the chart when it comes to actual profit and loss.

FIGURE 10-7

Renko Chart with Countertrend Trade for KLA-Tencor Corporation, Daily

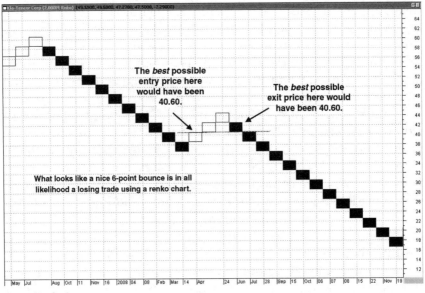

The *best* possible entry price here would have been 40.60.

The *best* possible exit price here would have been 40.60.

What looks like a nice 6-point bounce is in all likelihood a losing trade using a renko chart.

Source: MetaStock

SUMMARY

Renko charts use only the closing price, which eliminates noise or insignificant price movement. New bricks are drawn when a predetermined price level has been breached as determined by the chartist. Renko charts are very effective at

- Showing the price trend
- Revealing support and resistance levels

Drawbacks of using renko charts include the following:

- There is no usable time axis.
- Volume is not used.
- Windows or gaps are not evident on the chart.

Altering the brick size on a renko chart can change its appearance to the point where congestion areas or support and resistance levels may appear or disappear. Setting the brick size is a key element in making effective use of these charts. One method uses the Average True Range over a set period. Another method uses the actual price of the stock or commodity in its computation.

When one is trading by using renko charts, countertrend or whipsaw moves that consist of three or four bricks in the same direction may not be as profitable as they appear on the chart because of the amount of price action that could occur before a new brick is drawn. As always, it comes down to actual entry and exit prices when one is figuring profit or loss, not the appearance of bricks on a chart.

CHAPTER 11

Kagi Charts

Kagi charts are presented third in this sequence of candlestick cousins because their construction consists of a combination of the three-line break and renko methods. The Japanese word *kagi* refers to an old-fashioned key with an L-shaped head, which is a pattern that is visible in these charts. Because kagi charts are similar to a combination of the two previously discussed charting methodologies, one would be correct in surmising that a kagi chart also uses only closing prices, does not use volume or show windows, or have a meaningful time axis.

The basis of the kagi style of charting lies in its reflection of the trend by using a series of thick or thin lines to demonstrate when buyers or sellers are in control. Thicker lines show that price is making higher highs and higher lows (uptrend), and thinner lines show that price is making lower highs and lower lows (downtrend). Buy signals are given when the line changes from thin to thick, and sell signals when the line changes from thick to thin. There are also deeper trend analysis signals that are given by price movement, which we will examine in this chapter. Figure 11-1 shows a kagi chart.

FIGURE 11-1

Kagi Chart Example

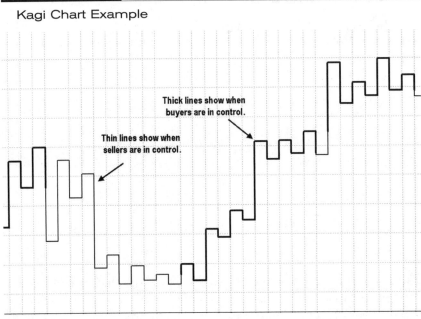

Source: MetaStock

CONSTRUCTING A KAGI CHART

Constructing a kagi chart is similar to constructing a renko chart in that a threshold value has to be breached for a new line to be drawn. As with renko charts, the threshold value is referred to as a reversal amount in many charting software packages. I find this misleading since not every violation of that value results in an actual reversal. These values are set by the chartist and can be set to either points or percentage. The hypothetical price scenario presented here starts at a price of $1 and uses a one-point threshold, as is depicted in Figure 11-2. The horizontal lines between vertical lines drawn on the chart are known as inflection lines.

Price begins at point A, using the starting point of 1. Price then rallies 2.25 up to 3.25, but just as with renko charts, the line is only up to 3 since it is drawn in one-point increments. This means that for the new line to be extended past 3, the closing price must exceed 4. Price then declined to 1.95, which caused a new line to

FIGURE 11-2

Kagi Chart Construction

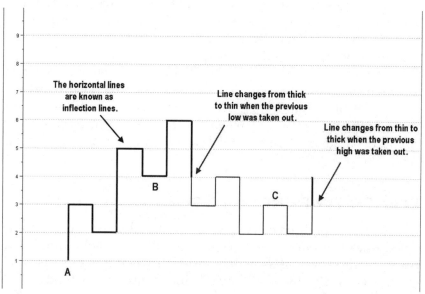

Source: MetaStock

be drawn to the 2 level since the close was 1 or more below the previous line at 3. Notice also that the line remained thick since no previous low price was violated. This left 2 as the new point of reference. From here, nothing would be drawn until price moved to 3 or higher or to 1 or lower.

After the decline to 1.95, price declined to 1.75, rallied to 2.10, and then declined to 1.80, which meant nothing was drawn on the chart since price did not break above 3 or below 1 (each is one point away from our reference point of 2). Price then rallied to 5.50, which necessitated a line being drawn up to 5, with 5 becoming the new reference point. Price declined to 3.95, which was more than one point below the previous line at 5, and so a line was drawn down to 4. The line still remained thick since no previous low price was violated. Price then rallied one more time to 6, which meant that a new line was drawn from 4 to 6. After the rally to 6, price declined to 3. Note how the line changed from thick to thin since the decline to 3 took out the previous swing low at 4 (point B). This showed that selling action was strong enough to break the series of higher highs and higher lows. Price then worked its way lower before rallying to 4 off the low at 2 to take out the previous swing high at 3 (point C). Once the swing high at C was taken out, the line changed from thin to thick again.

Remember, until the threshold level is taken out in either direction, nothing is plotted on the chart, which means that the daily noise of insignificant price movements is filtered out. Lines change from thick to thin when a previous swing low is taken out and change from thin to thick when a previous swing high is taken out.

POINTS OR PERCENTAGE?

When one is plotting a kagi chart, a decision has to be made whether to use points or percentage as the threshold value. The points method was used widely in Japan when these charts were introduced in the 1800s as it was a much simpler method to use than the cumbersome, time-consuming method of computing percentage changes from the reference value. However, with the technology available today, percentage changes are calculated easily by using charting software.

The difference between the two methods is that the point method probably will have to be adjusted as a stock appreciates in value. For example, a one-point move on a $30 stock is much less significant than a one-point move on a $3 stock. Using the percentage method, in contrast, allows for a consistent percentage amount to be used, and this will cause the actual threshold point values to expand and contract as price moves higher or lower. This makes longer-term analysis more meaningful in situations in which the price of a stock or commodity can double or triple. The chart of Apple Inc. in Figure 11-3 shows the difference between the two-point and 2 percent methods as price doubled from 175 to 350 from September 2009 to March 2011.

Note that there are fewer signals in the 2 percent chart because a 2 percent move on a stock in the price range of 175 to 350 is much more meaningful than a two-point move. Percent versus points

FIGURE 11-3

Kagi Percent versus Points on a Higher-Priced Stock: Apple Inc., Daily

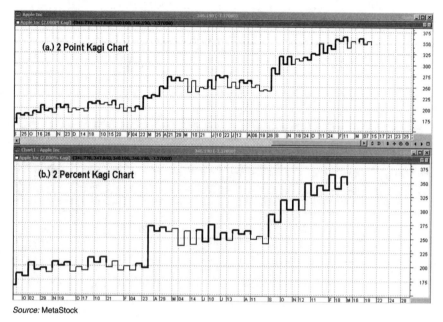

Source: MetaStock

has a much different effect on lower-priced stocks. The chart of Starbucks Corporation in Figure 11-4 shows the difference between one-point and 1 percent kagi chart as Starbucks was putting in its 2008 low. Notice in this case that the percentage method has many more signals because a 1 percent move on a single-digit stock yields a much smaller threshold than does a full one-point move.

Although these illustrations were formulated to show the difference between the two methods, I prefer using a percentage method with a higher setting of 4 percent. This setting reduces whipsaw signals on lower-priced stocks while making sure that reversals are meaningful on higher-priced stocks. Using the higher percentage setting also allows larger degree trends to be the focus. The examples from this point forward will use a threshold value of 4 percent.

FIGURE 11-4

Kagi Percent versus Points on a Lower-Priced Stock:
Starbucks Corporation, Daily

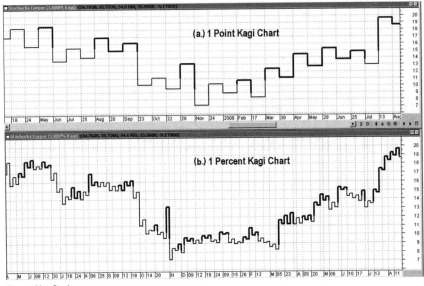

Source: MetaStock

KAGI CHARTS AND TRENDS

Kagi charts visually enhance trend analysis because of their transition from thick to thin lines and vice versa. The change in thickness of the plotted lines more closely resembles a three-line break chart in that the width is changed on the basis of price action taking out a previous high or low. As the examples above have shown, downtrends are made up predominantly of thin lines and uptrends are made up predominantly of thick lines. The chart of the Nasdaq Composite Index in Figure 11-5 shows a 4 percent kagi chart from its 2007 high to spring 2011. After the 2007 high, price retreated, causing a change from a thick line to a thin line. The initial countertrend rally in 2008 (on the left side of the chart) ran into resistance at the inflection line drawn off the two prior thick line lows (the dotted lines). After that brief rally caused the price line to transition back to thick, a new decline began that resulted

FIGURE 11-5

Kagi Chart Trends: Nasdaq Composite Index, Daily

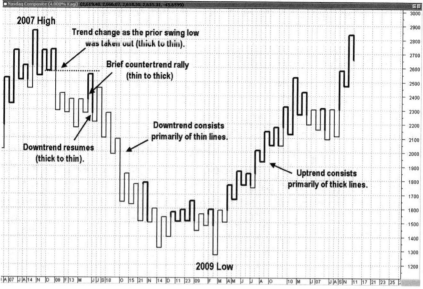

Source: MetaStock

in a series of thin lines as price declined. After the 2009 low in the center bottom of the chart, a series of higher highs and higher lows began that are shown by the thick lines.

KAGI CHARTS AND TREND REVERSALS

Trends are obvious in looking at a kagi chart, but what does it take to form a meaningful trend change? In the previous examples, short-term trading signals are evident as the line transitions from thick to thin and vice versa. That may be fine for shorter-term traders who want to trade the swings, but what about those who want to hold positions and ride the trend? The visual aspect of kagi charts allows a trader to see trend transitions as they are developing. Firm signals are given as the trend changes to allow longer-term traders to enter the market with confidence that a meaningful trend change has occurred. The daily chart of Microsoft Corporation in Figure 11-6 shows a trend transition at the February–March 2009 low.

Note on the left side of the chart that Microsoft Corporation was making a series of lower highs and lower lows until the low at point A in February 2009. The final, thick line reactionary high before the low at point A (point X) is an important part of our analysis. A dashed line has been drawn straight across from that high. After the low at point A, two consecutive higher lows were posted at point B and point C. Note that the point C low occurred on a thicker line, which showed that price strength was building as price remained well above the low at point B. After the low at point C, the line remained thick as price rallied up to the resistance line drawn from the swing high at point X (the dotted line). After the encounter with overhead resistance, price violated the low at point D, which caused the line to transition back to thin

FIGURE 11-6

Kagi Trend Change for Microsoft Corporation, Daily

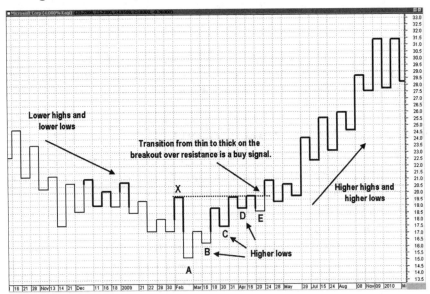

Source: MetaStock

at the point E low. After that brief pullback, price pushed higher through the resistance formed at point X (the dotted line). Once the line changed back to thick as it cleared resistance, a buy signal was given.

One valid question to ask is, Why wasn't the string of higher lows broken at the point E low? The reason is that coming off a downtrend, one must pay attention to the thin line lows at points A, B, and E. Since Microsoft was coming off a downtrend, the thin line lows are what mattered until the high at point X was taken out with a thick line. The reason for this is that since the thin inflection lines represent the action of sellers, the pattern of higher lows posted by the thin lines showed that selling pressure was weakening.

One of the drawbacks to the kagi charting method is the timing of the signals in a range-bound or trendless market. Just as with any other signal system, whipsaw signals are part of the game and can never be eliminated totally. In this environment, as price moves sideways, the timing of the signals many times can get a trader long near range tops and short near range bottoms. There also can be numerous very short-term signals within the range (away from the boundaries) that can lead to unnecessary losses. The chart of Agnico Eagle Mines Limited in Figure 11-7 shows how a sideways period from October 2002 through December 2005 could have resulted in a series of losses as Agnico Eagle Mines gave numerous signals within the trading range. This example illustrates the point, as discussed in Chapter 8, that one should be aware of the point at which trading signals occur. Was a buy signal generated just below larger-degree resistance, or was a sell signal generated just above larger-degree support? The same thing applies to kagi charts. If a buy signal is given near the top of the trading range, for example, wait until the top of the range is broken before acting on the signal.

KAGI CHARTS AND SUPPORT AND RESISTANCE

Just as with three-line break and renko charts, kagi charts are excellent at showing support and resistance areas because of the elimination of inconsequential price movements. The elimination

FIGURE 11-7

Kagi Range-Bound Market for Agnico Eagle Mines Limited, Daily

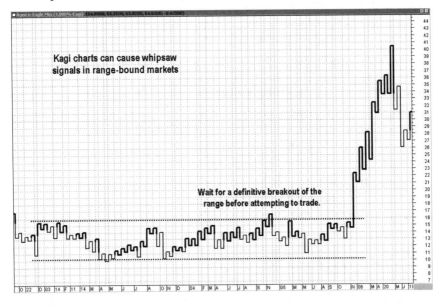

Source: MetaStock

of price noise allows important support and resistance areas to be exposed more easily. Kagi charts also allow for the drawing of longer-term trendlines, which can help keep longer-term traders on the right side of the market. The chart of Semiconductor HOLDR in Figure 11-8 illustrates the use of trendlines and support and resistance levels as aids in determining the overall trend and also in interpreting trading signals.

The chart begins at the June 2007 top. As price moved lower, forming lower highs and lower lows, a trendline could be drawn over the tops of the swing highs to create the downsloping resistance line. After the June 2007 top, support formed at the first reactionary low off which a horizontal dotted line was drawn. It was the break of this level at point A where a solid trend continuation signal was given as the low was violated in addition to the transition in the width of the line from thick to thin. Price then

FIGURE 11-8

Kagi Support and Resistance for Semiconductor HOLDR, Daily

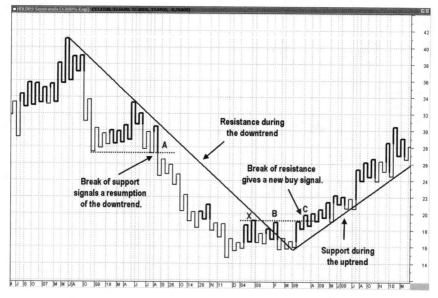

Source: MetaStock

continued lower as all price bounces were contained by the solid resistance line until it was broken to the upside at point B. This was an indication that a trend change might be near. Note that just as in the trend change shown in Figure 11-6, a resistance line was drawn off the top of the final reactionary high before the price bottomed in November 2008 (point X). This level provided enough resistance to turn prices lower at point B. After a mild decline and some sideways action, price finally broke through the resistance level formed at point X to begin a new uptrend. After the buy signal at point C, a new upward-sloping support line could be drawn connecting the lows as price moved higher.

Support and resistance also can come in more subtle forms in which larger-degree trends may not be as apparent. The chart of Intel Corporation in Figure 11-9 illustrates how a simple support line connecting reactionary lows can help confirm a larger-degree

FIGURE 11-9

Kagi Support and Resistance for Intel Corporation, Daily

Source: MetaStock

sell signal. In many cases, new chart readers train their eyes to look only for the places where major trendlines or horizontal support or resistance lines can be drawn. Learning to look for support and resistance in other places can enhance your trading success.

Note in the chart that the three reactionary lows at points 1, 2, and 3 were connected to form a valid support line. Once that support line was violated at point A, the sell signal was validated on two levels. First, the width of the line transitioned from thick to thin, and second, the price action violated the support line. This was all occurring within the larger-degree downtrend, as shown by the solid downsloping resistance line connecting point 4 and point B. Price reversed higher off the February 2009 low and moved higher until the previous resistance line was violated. Price then retreated slightly until it found support at point B. This once again illustrates that what was once resistance is now support. Price then continued higher into point C, where it ran into resistance. That resistance level was formed by the reactionary high at point 4, off which a horizontal dotted line was drawn.

The purpose of this example is to demonstrate that there are many support and resistance levels in a chart that can fit together to provide an accurate picture of what price action can be expected on the basis of trader behavior in the past. Changes in trader behavior create tremendous trading opportunities.

KAGI TERMINOLOGY

As with other Japanese charting methods, there are a couple of terms one should become acquainted with in using kagi charts. What have been referred to until now as reactionary highs and lows are in kagi terminology shoulders and waists. A shoulder is an inflection line or resistance point off a prior high, and a waist is an inflection line or support level off a prior low. Short-term sell signals are given when waists transition from thick to thin. Short-term buy signals are given when shoulders transition from thin to thick. Figure 11-10 illustrates shoulders, waists, and their signals. The signals generated in each case are more meaningful if they break a support or resistance level that consists of more

FIGURE 11-10

Shoulders and Waists

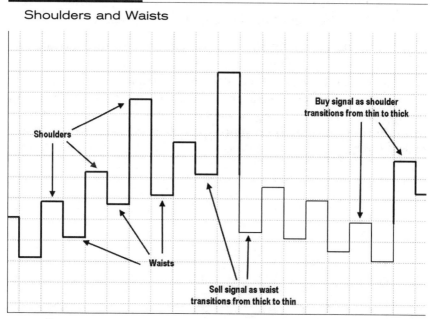

Source: MetaStock

than one shoulder or waist. For example, the sell signal shown in Figure 11-10 was formed after price broke down through the previous three thick-lined rising waists. That gave way to a steady but modest decline. The buy signal at the right of the chart also occurred as a new thick-lined shoulder was formed above the previous three thin-lined falling shoulders.

SUMMARY

Just like three-line break and renko charts, a kagi chart uses only the closing price in its construction. Kagi charts reflect the price trend with a series of thick (uptrend) or thin (downtrend) lines. The advantages and drawbacks of kagi charts are the same as those of renko charts.

Kagi charts are very effective at

- Showing the price trend
- Revealing support and resistance levels

Drawbacks of using kagi charts include the following:

- There is no usable time axis.
- Volume is not used.
- Windows or gaps are not evident on the chart.

Some discretion by the chartist is required in choosing the points or percentage method for the threshold value. The percentage method is preferred because it expands and contracts with price values as stocks and/or commodities sometimes can double or triple in price. Shoulders and waists are terms that refer to the inflection lines representing support (waists) or resistance (shoulders).

Index